W9-CFP-196

Dedication

To my mother, Eleanor Wann Ferguson, who first introduced me to the joys of embroidery, sewing, and needlework of all kinds. I remember many happy childhood hours spent with her — with fabric or needle in hand. Her enthusiasm and the way she shared it with me began a life-long adventure in design and the business of creativity.

To my late father, Walter Johnson, whose idea of a humorous moniker for his only child was "Muttonhead", because her hair was so curly she looked like a little lamb. Dad's example of steadfast love enfolds me daily.

To my incredible husband, Geoff. His love, support, encouragement, and willingness to eat carryout makes it possible for me to spend the time necessary to develop the concepts and the systems for turning those concepts into something to share with others. I couldn't do it without him!

To the wonderful Muttonhead team: Sandy, Debby, Beth, Suzan, and Heidi. Your generosity, enthusiasm, and willingness to share your stitching talents made this a reality — even if you occasionally questioned the wisdom of my color choices.

And, especially, to you, the special person reading this book. I hope you find joy in the designs and color arrangements, then share that joy with your special someone. Without you, the joy stops here!

Acknowledgments

Heartfelt thanks to Julie Stephani, acquisitions editor at Krause who saw the potential in this book proposal, and Christine Townsend, editor, who has been a great cheerleader during the formative stages of this book.

Special thanks to Wendy Woomer at Baby-2-Teen Furniture store in Manassas, Virginia, for allowing photographer Deborah Del Tejo and me to invade the store on short notice to use their fabulous furniture and accessories for many photos in this book.

Thanks to June Mellinger at Brother Sewing Machine Company, who has sent a steady stream of machines to us with which to experiment and construct quilts over the years.

Thanks to Deborah Del Tejo at Moon Shadow Photography, Manassas, Virginia, who took all the photographs in this book.

Table of Contents

Inspiration

Teaching yourself to draw inspiration from things you encounter every day sounds just too simple, doesn't it? And yet, it's so very true. This collection of adorable quilts has been inspired by embroidery motifs from the '30s, '40s, and '50s.

It's fun to browse antique stores, sales, and shows, where a seemingly endless supply of goodies — doilies, dresser scarves, pillowcases, tea towels, handkerchiefs, as well as books, catalogs, iron-on transfers, and magazines showing designs for embellishing a multiplicity of surfaces — provides a wealth of color and design inspiration.

We've included a designer note with each quilt explaining what inspired the motif and how we adapted it for use on the quilt.

Materials and Supplies

Fabric is so important to successful quilting, we sometimes compose a design inspired by the fabric itself. Of course, 100 percent cotton is preferred. We seldom, if ever, wash the fabrics before stitching, but then we use high-quality cottons and our quilts are intended for display, while your quilt will be snuggled, loved — and laundered repeatedly.

If you've chosen bargain fabrics with obviously low thread counts (fewer threads per inch equals more space between fibers and a high possibility of shrinkage), please consider pre-washing.

Because I know you don't want to wash, dry, and iron all those fabrics, see the chart on page 6 to guide you.

Muttonhead's Guidelines for When to Pre-wash Fabrics:

◆ In general, higher-quality fabrics shrink less than lower-quality fabrics.

◆ If your quilt will be hung on a wall, you probably don't need to pre-wash and dry fabrics. If, however, it will be laundered repeatedly, you probably do need to pre-wash.

◆ Dyes and mordants (the stuff that makes the dye stick to the fibers) in dark fabrics, such as indigo and black, can irritate delicate skin of any age. If your quilt will come in snuggle contact with skin, you may want to pre-wash fabrics.

◆ Babies spit up (among other things), children spill (and then wipe up with whatever is handy), and teenagers … well, you get the idea. If your quilt will be subjected to the rigors of use, abuse, and love, it must be able to make repeated trips through the laundry. Pre-wash!

Tools

The choice and condition of scissors and thread nippers are important for cleanly clipping threads and cutting fabrics. In real life (meaning yours and mine), fabric scissors are seldom used exclusively for fabric. In a moment of great need, we'll all reach for the nearest cutting utensil to open the box or cut the duct tape. And there's no chance I'll be hypocritical and advocate having scissors sharpened once a year. There are a few things, however, that you can do to improve the performance of scissors' cutting edges and extend their lives.

Muttonhead's Tips for Healthy Scissors

◆ Clean any sticky gunk from the blades with an adhesive solvent, such as Un-Du™ on a paper towel or napkin.

◆ Cut through waxed paper several times to revitalize blades. This isn't a cure for nasty nicks or just plain dull scissors, but it will perk up a slow blade.

◆ Stubborn spots may be rubbed gently with steel wool. Again, this won't heal nicks, but it will improve performance.

◆ When all else fails, treat all of your scissors to a trip to the sharpener. Many fabric stores have a repair person in the store once a month or so who can give all cutting utensils a new edge — at a modest charge.

Rotary Cutter System

Rotary cutters, along with their companions, self-healing mats and acrylic rulers, have revolutionized quilting. They've made it possible for quilters to easily cut several layers of fabric at a time – with a clean, straight edge. These handy tools instantly made strip-piecing popular, and innovative designers quickly developed wonderful techniques for utilizing them.

Using rotary cutters is optional in creating the quilts in this book, but they will make the process of cutting strips and blocks quicker and cleaner. See the basic technique illustrated on page 19.

Muttonhead's Tips for Choosing a Rotary Cutter System

◆ Purchase a mat large enough to comfortably accommodate fabric yardage. The bigger the better! If you do a lot of cutting, you may want to consider a mat large enough to cover the entire work surface. These can be ordered through your local quilt shop (and I do mean "ordered" … they probably will not have them on hand).

◆ Rotary cutters come in a variety of sizes. Smaller wheels are great for cutting delicate fabric, one-fold fabric, curves, etc. Larger wheels are needed for cutting multiple layers.

◆ Blades should be smooth and free of nicks. Any distortion in the blade will cause threads to be skipped. We recommend replacing blades often, and with care.

◆ Avoid the temptation to use the rotary cutter on wallpaper and cardboard. Or, if you can't resist, dedicate a rotary cutter strictly for those purposes — and plan to change the blade frequently.

◆ Acrylic rulers should be at least 22" to 24", long enough to cover fabric folded selvage to selvage.

◆ Rulers should have lines marked every 1/4" for easy reading along the length of the ruler.

◆ Some rulers have angles marked, as well. These can be very helpful when cutting fabrics in geometric shapes.

◆ The acrylic-ruler surface is smooth and will slide. Our favorite ruler is more than 18 years old and has small ridges on the fabric side to gently grip fibers. It has been used so much, the paint has worn off the lines and numbers.

Thread

When it comes to thread, don't skimp on quality. Threads really do make a difference. Quality thread is smooth when you hold it up to the light, with few fuzzies to clog the machine. Quality thread helps form even stitches, rarely breaks from flaws in the fiber, and feeds evenly for fewer skipped stitches. Its strength and durability make it the *real* bargain — not the "4 for $1" special offers on thread with a brand name you don't recognize!

A debate has raged for years among quilters regarding the choice of 100 percent cotton threads, 100 percent polyester threads, cotton-wrapped polyester, rayon, monofilament, etc. They each have a place in special situations. For our purposes, we recommend all-purpose, cotton-wrapped polyester for construction. For smooth, lustrous, satin stitches, the Muttonhead team routinely uses a combination of rayon thread in the upper machine and matching color of all-purpose thread in the bobbin.

A word about monofilament threads: We recommend monofilament threads for quilting *only* when the finished quilt will not come in contact with delicate skin. Even the finest monofilament can cause irritation if a stitch comes loose or an end is not clipped flush with the fabric surface. When we do use monofilament thread, we prefer one with a thickness about equal to a strand of hair.

Iron

The overall look of a quilt is greatly affected by the use of an iron. We press with steam and an iron set to a temperature appropriate for cotton fabrics. Nothing beats the crispness of a quilt top with seam allowances pressed throughout the construction process — and no quilt is considered finished without the final pressing of the binding. What a difference that simple step makes!

Sewing Machine

It isn't necessary to have a fancy sewing machine. If your machine can crank out smooth, well-made, straight and zigzag stitches, you can make any quilt in this book. So, what are the secrets to top-grade stitches in your machine? Make sure your sewing machine is clean, its tension is well-balanced, and use a new needle.

Knowing how to handle such routine maintenance is like being on a "first-name basis" with your machine. You need to know how to clean and care for the machine — and when to take it to a professional. Find the manual and read it; it's full of dandy information to keep the machine humming along.

Muttonhead Tips for Getting to Know Your Sewing Machine

◆ If you've never had the machine checked, you might want to spend a little money ($50 or so for manual machines) and have it professionally cleaned and tuned (just like your car).

◆ When did you last change the needle? If the machine is still sporting the needle it had when you brought it home, it's time for a new one. We recommend a new needle for each quilt.

◆ Invest in a basting brush — a new one, not one from the kitchen drawer. The long bristles are perfect for reaching thread dust in tight spaces.

◆ Canned air is great for blowing thread dust from impossible-to-reach spaces.

◆ Thread dust in the bobbin assembly and between tension disks of older machines can be the cause of skipped and uneven stitches.

◆ Does your machine talk to you? Mine all make subtle little sounds when something is amiss. One has a recognizable click when the bobbin is about to run out of thread. Another one makes a tiny cough when there are thread-feeding problems and the thread is about to break. The trusty older machine moans at me when the needle is straining to pierce the fabrics — a sure sign the project needs a larger needle. So, listen to your machine; it may have something to tell you.

◆ Make sure you know how to thread the upper machine and bobbin. It only takes a few minutes (after finding the manual) to check the threading sequence, while an improperly threaded machine can cause a lifetime of annoying symptoms.

Batting

Batting is the "peanut butter" in the quilt "sandwich." Some people like crunchy, some smooth; others like to add jelly or marshmallow fluff. We've found the same to be true of quilt batting. Each member of the Muttonhead team has a favorite batting, depending on the type of quilt and the way it will be used.

Sandy

"I like needle-punched cotton batting best because of the nice feel it gives to a quilt. My second choice is 80 percent/20 percent cotton/polyester blend. Both allow you to iron-baste the quilt sandwich together, making it easy to baste or pin. On small projects you don't have to pin at all!"

Debby

"When I want an old-fashion look, I like 100 percent cotton batting. It machine-quilts well and has the flat finish of a quilt made decades ago. Cotton batting works well for patchwork quilts when you are stitching in the ditch and just want moderate definition. Cotton batting also has natural warmth.

"For appliqué quilts, and for those with more definition around the appliquéd shapes, I like polyester batting. Polyester batting gives quilts a fluffy, comforter look, especially those with higher loft. The only drawback with polyester batting is the pressure foot sometimes gets stuck in the fibers when you're working around the edges."

Beth Hannum

"When constructing small-to-medium wall hangings, I prefer a brand-name fusible batting. It allows the quilter to get right to quilting and finishing stages of the project. Fusible batting makes it possible to actually complete a 'weekend' project in a weekend!

"For larger projects, I like 90"-wide batting-by-the-yard, available in most fabric and quilt stores. It's smooth, stable, and produces a quilt sandwich free of bumps and bulges. Those times when you want the quilt to look like Great Grandma's, cotton batting is great."

Suzan

"The fuse-on-both-sides batting fuses tightly, but looks a little rumpled (rumples are supposed to wash out). It's very easy to work with because it bonds firmly, and eliminates the need for pins.

"The fuse-on-one-side batting still needs pins around the edges and I use a basting spray between the batting and whichever (top or bottom) that isn't fused. This creates a fairly firm bonding between layers.

"Both types of fusible battings are thin and firm without much loft. Overall, fusible battings make handling the quilt sandwich while machine quilting easy, but there is not much loft and therefore little definition even after the quilting is done. I like the look of a thicker batting because it gives the quilted shapes much more personality.

"I sometimes use a regular, mid-loft batting and hold the sandwich together with basting spray and pins while machine quilting. This is easy enough with a snuggle-size quilt; a larger project would still require basting with pins or thread. It should be noted that basting spray allows the work to be repositioned and disappears after three or four days."

Heidi

"I prefer June Tailor's fusible batting in the pre-cut rolls when making wall hangings or crib-size quilts, but non-fusible batting for a bed-size quilt, because it is easier to handle under the arm of the sewing machine when quilting." (Heidi is a woman of few words.)

Beth Wheeler

"I've worked with every type of batting imaginable: wool, silk, cotton, synthetic, and cotton/synthetic blends. Wool is a novelty and very expensive. It also requires heavy quilting to prevent bunching. Silk has a drape that can't be equaled, but is very expensive and used mostly for quilted art clothing. If you are considering either wool or silk, don't forget the allergy factor for both the quilter and the recipient of the quilt.

"The new cotton batting on the market is wonderful, giving heirloom-quality quilts a vintage look with the way they accept needling. (The true beauty is revealed after the quilt has been washed at least once.)

"Synthetic batting is readily available in a variety of lofts, offering ease of handling and a choice of finished looks. For hand quilting, low-loft batting is a good choice, as the low bulk facilitates small stitches. I like medium-loft for machine quilting. It handles well under the machine and has a soft poof around the stitches. High-loft batting can be a problem to maneuver under the machine and is better left for hand-tied comforters.

"Cotton/synthetic blends are a dream for constructed clothing. I often stitch strips of constructed fabric directly to the bonded batting. It offers no-stretch support, superior shaping for jackets and bodices, and, when lined, holds all bobbin stitches invisibly in the completed piece.

"The new fusible battings offer the convenience of holding the quilt sandwich together without tedious basting — a real time-saver if you like the feel of the finished quilt. I like the dense feel under the machine while quilting and the way the finished quilt handles. The new fusibles are available in cotton and synthetic and at least two lofts — low and high."

Controlling the Design

Color

From the Quilter's Point of View ….

Color can be a scary thing to beginners and experienced quilters alike. Color placement makes all the difference in a quilt, but it's impossible to judge proper placement until the quilt is complete. What's a quilter to do?

Many books are written, and classes and workshops taught on the study of color and its use in quilt design. By all means, read the books, experience the workshops, try the color wheels … but at some point, you have to lay down the notes and touch the fabric.

What to do at that point? Work with colors you like! Begin with a small selection of one- or two-color combinations, and work on small pieces to build confidence. Then, slowly, step outside of your comfort zone of color combinations and try something new.

Designing 20 quilts for this book allowed the Muttonhead team to try a variety of color fantasies — and what fun it was! We began with the basics: pink and blue; red, white, and blue; primary red, yellow, blue, and green; red and white, and so on. Then, we moved beyond the basics to try yellow and lavender, turquoise and orange, peach and blue, purple and red. Each time we tried something new, we tried to analyze why we liked the combination. Some color combinations evoked feelings of peace and security; others stimulated curiosity or a sense of fantasy … and still others seemed just plain cheerful. We noticed they all made all of us feel good!

Out of the experimentation grew the thought that, like us adults, babies respond to color; perhaps we could develop a plan beneficial to babies with limited vision, Down's Syndrome, those with crack-addicted mothers, autistic children, and any baby who might benefit from additional visual stimulation.

Our research led to the discovery of many groups that make quilts for babies with special needs. We share these on page 125 and encourage you to contact those of interest. These worthy causes serve many innocents in need of love and a little kindness — and the groups also welcome donations of time, fabric, patterns, and money.

Please, check with your local Better Business Bureau to verify the validity of any organization to which you give money. We are not advocating any one group — just encouraging you to give of your resources and talents to those who need it. You'll find yourself receiving as much joy as you give.

From Baby's Point of View ….

Babies respond to color. Unless she (boy and girl babies respond to the loving touch of quilts, but we're using the feminine pronoun in this case) has a visual impairment, Baby can see from birth. As she grows, Baby will take in large amounts of information about the world around her, which in turn will stimulate brain development and lead to physical accomplishments, such as sitting, rolling over, crawling, and walking.

How does Baby's sight develop? Unlike hearing, which is fully mature by the end of the first month, vision develops gradually. At birth, vision is fuzzy, though she can make out light, shapes, and movement. She can see only as far as about 8" to 15" — just enough to clearly make out the face of the person holding her. Your face is the most interesting thing to Baby at this age, followed by high-contrast, black-and-white items such as a checkerboard. It's a good thing to put in a lot of eye-to-eye contact at this stage. Bring Baby close to you, establish eye contact, and watch her track your movements so her brain gets used to telling her eyes that this is something to see. Baby's eyesight will gradually improve until she is about eight months old, when she will see just as well as you do.

So, why colors? Babies see color from birth, but they have a difficult time distinguishing differences between similar tones, such as red and orange. Beginning at two months and continuing through to four months of age, color differences become clearer, and Baby starts to distinguish like shades. She will probably begin to show a preference for bright, primary colors, and more detailed and complicated designs and shapes. You can encourage this by letting Baby look at bright pictures or toys. During this time, she will also be perfecting object-tracking skills.

At four months, Baby will begin to develop depth perception. This new visual development allows her to grab for things, such as hair and earrings, more accurately.

At five months, she will have already learned to distinguish between similar bold colors, and will begin to sort out subtle differences in pastels.

At eight months, Baby's vision will be almost adult-like in its clarity and depth perception. Although her close-range vision is still better, she will begin to recognize people and objects across the room.

What You Can Do to Help Your Baby's Developing Sight

Encourage Baby's interest in primary colors and pastels as she gets older. Primary-colored quilts, mobiles, and posters will be important tools in helping to develop visual acuity. Babies cannot take in too much stimulation, but be aware of periods when Baby is more attentive, and use these times to help her development. If Baby is distracted, it is best to use this time as a quiet time, because she won't be focused on whatever you are trying to show her.

At about 18 months, a child begins to notice similarities and differences in shape, size, and texture. She also develops the ability to differentiate among colors. It will be a while longer before she's able to name the colors, although most children can name at least one color at 36 months. Meanwhile, she will enjoy practicing, adding new colors to her repertoire. She may surprise you by knowing and identifying colors even if she cannot name them verbally.

When you are out together, play pointing and matching games. Say: "Can you see the red flower?" and wait to see if she can identify it, before pointing it out. Point to her shirt color and ask if she sees something else that is the same color. Toddlers love looking at picture books of objects organized by shape and color. Start by asking her to identify things by sight, saying, "Can you show me the red square?" and let her point to it.

As she gets older, you can reverse the game. Ask her what color something is when you point at it. When she's wrong, don't correct her or pretend she's right, but instead say the correct name in an encouraging tone.

When to Be Concerned About Your Baby's Vision

Babies should be screened for vision problems regularly — starting at birth and continuing at each checkup. If spotted early enough, most vision deficiencies can usually be corrected. You can spot the more obvious signs of problems, such as difficulty focusing or tracking an object. If you see this, tell your pediatrician. A few other warning signs are: Trouble moving one or both eyes in all directions, crossed eyes, eyes that tend to turn out. If you see any of these signs, tell your pediatrician.

Visual Impairments

Children who have a visual impairment can still benefit from color stimulation. For instance, an organization called "Quilts from Caring Hands" makes and distributes tactile quilts to children who are blind or who have very poor vision. The quilts incorporate not only contrasting colors, but also patches that are made from textured fabrics. When children touch the quilts, they can easily feel the difference in textures and when the contrast in colors is very apparent, those who have some sight can differentiate among different areas on the quilt. Being able to touch and feel the different textures contributes toward their ability to learn Braille.

The quilts are used as teaching tools, as well as for comfort for the children. There are generally two or three pockets on each quilt that can hide a squeaky toy or can be used as another place for small hands to explore. Colors are high-contrast, such as black and white or neon colors, which stimulate what little sight a child may have. Small patterns such as checks, zigzags, swirls, and stripes can also stimulate the eye to move if there is any sight at all. The quilt back is generally red flannel that can serve as a surface on which to place a toy to see if the child can locate it. While a sighted child is visually stimulated to explore surroundings and to move out of the comfort zone, the hope is that the different textures on these special quilts will make the visually-impaired child curious to discover what is beyond her arm's length and move toward it.

The quilts in this book offer a variety of color combinations — some smooth and creamy, like sherbet, and others one can only describe as color crescendos. Don't let yourself fall into a color rut. Experiment and enjoy the rainbow in all its many variations.

Bridging

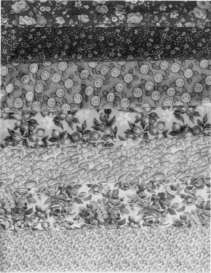

You'll see the term "bridging" used throughout this book and in Muttonhead patterns. "Bridging" refers to fabrics in colors, patterns, scales, and values to bridge the gap between two fabrics you'd like to use in a quilt.

Let's pretend we are choosing fabrics for a cobalt blue and golden yellow quilt. The photo on the left shows a collection of lovely medium-blue prints with a short range of values and a grouping of golden-yellow prints with a short range of values. They look nice, but they really have nothing to do with one another. They don't connect, because they

don't have a bridge.

Bridging fabrics are prints with both colors in them. The center photo shows yellow-and-blue prints with a variety of scale and value. Not all fabrics will do this successfully. In the group photographed, the two prints in the leftmost positions are of values that don't match the values of the blues or yellows.

The final selection of fabrics in the photo on the right includes blue, yellow, and yellow-and-blue prints in corresponding values.

Contrast

Before

After

After

Contrast in color intensity and saturation helps define shapes and separate them from the background. In the first version of the Elf Cottage, contrast between the background, cloud, sunshine, and border was not as marked as expected, and the shape didn't pop from the background.

To rectify this, we worked a dark-blue straight stitch along each side of the white satin stitches.

The Sunshine behaved in a similar manner. The yellow thread outlining the yellow sun face and rays just didn't set it apart from the border. Using a brighter red-orange thread set the shapes off nicely.

Value

Expressed as low, medium, or dark, the "value" of the fabric refers to the relative lightness or darkness of the print's effect. As a beginning quilter, I was instructed to squint my eyes to remove the color influence and look through my eyelashes at the lightness/darkness of the fabric.

It's All Relative

What do we mean by "relative lightness or darkness" of the print's effect? Look at the three photos in this example. We've chosen all blue

fabrics with little or no other colors to confuse the issue, enabling us to focus on value alone.

The same two fabrics are found in each collection, yet they play a different role in each group. In the first photo, the two repeating fabrics are the darkest-value in the group, and would perform well in an inner border to stop the design. In the second photo, the two repeating fabrics are right in the middle. In the last photo, they are the lightest-value fabrics and would be appropriate as background, piecing, or binding.

Scale

Scale refers to the proportional size of the print. To make a quilt sing, include prints representing a variety of scales: small, medium, and large.

All these prints have a dark-blue background and red flowers with green leaves. Now, look at the

way they "read." Some are dense, with tiny flowers set close together, while others are more airy, with larger flowers and more background showing among the blossoms.

Muttonhead Design Approach

The rather irreverent Muttonhead approach to quilt design began to evolve about 15 years ago. At the time, I was on a track as a serious, contemporary art-quilt designer, or so I thought. At some point, it became necessary to examine motives and re-define goals. Did I want to amaze and dazzle quilt audiences with a visual complexity of color and design? No, the goal was a little less lofty: To support my family, to bring joy (or at least a smile) to those who saw my work, and encourage others to experience the adventure for themselves.

To accomplish this, a major overhaul was needed. Cultivating joy and smiles when looking at quilts involved "cute," and thinking in the language of "cute" was neither native to me, nor had I been trained for it in a professional sense. I really had to work at it! What evolved, and is still evolving, is a process of looking at images the world considers cute. Children's books, needlecraft magazines from the 1900s to the present, decorating magazines, greeting cards, sales ads, and toy stores — all have become learning tools. The challenge is to identify those images I consider cute and analyze why I perceive them to be cute. That has led to the "cute factor" and "cute scale" in the world of Muttonhead.

Cute Factor and Cute Scale

What is it that makes something "cute"? A tilt of the head, a sweet expression on the face, childlike proportions of the character, fun colors, and prints all work together to create a "cute factor" in a quilt composition.

Like anyone learning something new in the world of art, I began by pouring over work of favorite artists and illustrators. Bessie Peace Smith, Bertha Corbet Melcher, Mary Engelbreit, Annie Lang, and Dianne J. Hook all became teachers, whether they knew it or not.

I practiced drawing their characters, emphasizing the features with the highest cute factor, and then changing them to suit myself. I experimented with raising and lowering the eyebrows (an especially expressive facial feature), bringing eyes closer together and farther apart, tilting the chin for an ingenuous look, working with the mouth to create different expressions, and adjusting the proportions for a pudgy, childlike look.

I cheerfully spent a small fortune on coloring books, clip art, iron-on transfers, vintage books, catalogs, and textiles. I drew and erased on a lot of sketchbooks, and threw away many less-than-successful attempts in the process of developing a formula that works.

Working with Many Prints

One way our designs achieve their signature cute factor is by using many different prints in a quilt composition. Quilters have lots of fabrics, usually many projects in the works at one time and many scraps. We set out to use snippets of many fabrics in a pleasing way. Each pattern in this book is calculated to use scraps, but we've also provided yardage requirements, in the event you prefer to use one print, rather than many.

We found some quilters actually resist using the last scrap of a favorite print in the event it will be needed at some time in the future. This quickly leads to overpopulation in the fabric-storage area — but quilters revel in the tactile and visual joy of fabric itself.

We offer ourselves as an example. We thought the challenge of making 20 quilts for this book, using only fabrics in our collection, would reduce the fabric population and make room for new acquisitions. Somehow, even after making 20 quilts, purchasing practically no fabric at all (well, almost no fabric at all), our wire-drawer fabric-storage system is still bulging with fabrics. Even with our rudimentary grasp of college math and physics, something isn't right about this equation. Okay; maybe we did purchase a few fabrics for the quilts in this book — but just a few!

 Muttonhead Tips for Working with Many Prints

◆ There are no "rules" when working with many prints. No fabric police will come knocking on the door, but there are guidelines to help you achieve the intended effect.

◆ Pick a main (anchor) fabric in color and motif to reflect the theme of your quilt. Add fabrics that coordinate with the anchor fabric in varying value, scale, and contrast. Add a stripe, plaid, dot, or check for variety. Include some bridging fabrics with elements of both colors to help the eye accept the transition from one color to another.

◆ Lay the chosen fabrics on a plain, flat surface and stand back far enough to see the fabrics as a unit. Do any fabrics stand out and not look right? Pull them out, or add another to create balance and serve as the bridge between the two.

◆ When assigning position to the fabrics in the composition, choose a light-value print for the background to add interest and allow for contrast between appliqué pieces and the background.

◆ The background print should not be so busy or bold as to take the eye away from the appliqué.

◆ If the print is the perfect color and scale, but just too bold, turn it to the "wrong" side.

◆ Choose a dark-value fabric for the inner border and binding to stop the design and complete the visual statement.

◆ When choosing fabrics for the outer border, use boldest or brightest fabrics selectively. Dominant colors or prints, such as yellow, can take over the quilt quickly. Use small pieces placed in a balanced arrangement around the quilt to make it sparkle.

◆ To prevent background fabrics, especially stripes, from "ghosting" through a white or white-on-white appliqué piece, use a second layer of white to line the first and create a more-opaque shape.

◆ Light-value fabrics come to the foreground and darker-value fabrics recede. So, when choosing fabrics for an appliqué with dimension or layers, you should choose dark-value fabrics for those elements toward the back of the composition and light-value fabrics for those in the front.

◆ This is supposed to be fun! Experiment with various combinations of fabrics. Pin swatches up on a bulletin board, or tape them to a doorframe or mirror so you can live with the combination for a few days. If you like the blend — go for it. If you don't, rearrange and try again. It's a lot easier to make adjustments now, rather than after the quilt top is stitched together.

◆ Use fabrics for binding and border elsewhere in the quilt to pull it all together. If they aren't repeated, those fabrics may appear out of context and as if they just don't "belong" to the quilt.

◆ We like action or interest in the borders! Choose from small block piecing, strip pieces, or an appliqué element moving out of the confines of its block or border.

Definition of a Solid

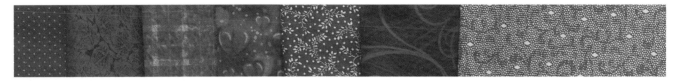

We readily admit to re-defining the word "solid" (always said with a wink). In our world, a solid is any print that doesn't read as an obvious print. To illustrate this slightly warped approach to fabric selection, we chose red-and-white prints for the photo. From a distance, the fabrics each appear to be solid red or variegated red, and we simply consider the amount of white or black an expression of value.

All the truly solid-color fabrics in the Muttonhead collection are at the bottom of the bins. We haven't used a true solid in years — other than an occasional polished cotton for a nose or skin.

Adding Variety to a Repeated-Block Design

Muttonhead has resisted the common repeated-block quilt design; we find it infinitely more fun to experiment with various ways to make repeated-block designs more interesting. We'll share several secrets with you, but challenge you to analyze each quilt composition in this book to determine how we added variety and to determine which will work in your own designs.

Block Position

    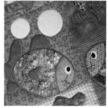 

One way to add variety is to vary the block position. Rotate the block or the design within the block to shift the focus of the motif. The Littlest Prop Plane quilt on page 28 is a charming example. This is a straight repeated-block design, with one exception — the plane in the lower left block has broken free from its block and is heading up the border! (We took the modern-day maxim "Think outside the box" literally.)

Wrong-Way Dragonfly (page 62) is another example. It changes only one block, but it makes a world of difference in the focus of this delightful quilt.

Let's look at **Peek-A-Boo Bunny** (page 44) as a third example of varying block position. The bunny is tilted at various angles in each block, while the bunny in the center block is chopped off at the bottom to make it appear to be peeking out over the top. We rate this approach high on the cute scale.

Adding Pieced Borders

The Cat's Meow on page 36 is a straight block arrangement, with kitties varied slightly. The real eye-catching feature on this quilt is the strip-pieced borders. The simple, strip-pieced outer borders, offset slightly to create angled stripes of varying widths and colors, emphasizes the quilt's colors while adding motion at the same time.

Varying Block Arrangement

Fish Out of School on page 40 adds a simple shifting of the block arrangement. Rather than each column of blocks lining up in even rows, the center column is offset by half a block. In this case, one block in both the first and last columns is split in half with one half of the block at the top of the column and the remaining half at the bottom. Additionally, the position of the fish is varied to immediately direct the eye to the two fish friends discovering one another.

We can't complete this discussion without looking at the adorable **Puppy Love** on page 48. This layout involves setting the blocks on point, adding triangles to bring the composition to a square. It punctuates the center with an inner border, and finishes with an elaborate scalloped outer border — a more-elaborate approach, to be sure.

Strip Piecing around Each Block

Another way to add interest to repeated-block compositions is to add simple strip-piecing around the blocks. For instance, **Wrong-Way Dragonfly** (page 62) uses simple sashing and corner blocks, while **Big-Mouth Frog** (page 32) stitches strips around each block, log-cabin style. **Tiptoe Scotties** on page 58 adds a single round of logs, but the reproduction fabrics provide a feeling of warm whimsy.

Simplify Construction to Match Your Time and Skills

We've used a number of strip-piecing combinations in borders. Some are more tedious than others, but none are really difficult. Please feel free to take a border design from one quilt and put it on another to adjust the construction to fit the time and skills with which you feel comfortable. Just be sure to adjust the fabric requirements accordingly.

The fun and adventure of mixing and matching elements to suit your own style is what personalizes each quilt. Enjoy the adventure!

Quilt Backs

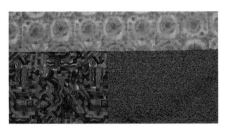

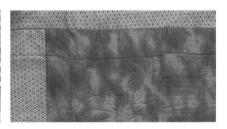

We love it when one piece of fabric doesn't cover the back of a quilt. The back becomes yet another surface on which to express ourselves. Remember, Baby is going to love, wallow in, clutch, and stain this quilt with a variety of body fluids. So, don't make this your finest creation … these quilts are meant to be loved and used.

Labels

Don't neglect to add a label with your name, the recipient's name, the title of the quilt or name of the block pattern, and the date. Although a quilt may not survive years of use, abuse, and love to become an heirloom, it's wonderful to see your loved one's name every day and remember their gift of time and loving stitches.

Much has been written about documenting quilts in recent years. As vintage quilts became recognized as folk art, the need for information about the quilt and quilter became obvious. Our quilt world would be all the richer if it included information about the women who made the quilts we admire today, along with the circumstances under which the quilts were made and/or given.

Some quilt conservators advocate stitching the quilter's name and date on the back, while others feel an applied label is best. We've waited for the development of a permanent ink, or a fabric, since Marjorie Croner's book Fabric Photos, describing the process of printing photos on fabric, was released in 1989. However, the inkjet industry tells us the technology used by these printers is currently dependent on inks with a viscosity only available in water-based products. That leaves us to the fabric — and now it's here. At Muttonhead, our labels are printed on ColorPlus™ fabric, a cotton fabric with a binder embedded in the fibers to make inkjet printer ink permanent in hand washing.

The fabric is impregnated with a chemical binder to bond inks to the fabric's fibers. Each sheet comes out of the package temporarily mounted to a sheet of paper to facilitate smooth feeding through the printer. Once in the printer, anyone with a photo, drawing, or graphics program on a home computer can print any image imaginable. Check the resources list at the back of the book for a mail-order source for ColorPlus. It's available in 100 percent cotton in various weights and sizes, plus rayon, silk, and kits for ties, purses, and more.

Respect Copyrights!

Just because we now have the technology to print any image on fabric, that doesn't mean we can. Beware of copyright issues and don't violate copyright laws. That means you may print any photo or drawing of your own creation, but not that of anyone's copyrighted artwork. Disney would frown on someone scanning Mickey Mouse or Winnie the Pooh and printing it on fabric for a pillow. Likewise, Uncle Sam would take a dim view of someone scanning or copying currency and printing it — even for personal use. And any photo taken by a professional photographer is copyrighted. The latter may grant permission for you to use the photos, but ask first.

Basic Techniques

Some techniques are used repeatedly throughout this book. Rather than repeat those technique instructions each time, we offer them here and refer back to them. Please feel free to substitute your favorite method for any of these.

For example, if you have another method for applying binding that's faster and easier than the one we use, by all means use it — and send it to me in care of Krause Publications!

Cutting Strips

A rotary cutter, self-healing mat, and acrylic ruler make quick work of cutting strips with clean, straight edges — provided fabric is cut at the correct angle.

A slice cut off the vertical/horizontal axis creates an uneven strip that will adversely affect strip piecing (see Figure 1).

Begin with a smooth piece of fabric; folds or crinkles cause irregularities in the strip. So, iron the fabric, if necessary. Fold the fabric in half lengthwise, with the fold toward you on the work surface and excess to the right (or to the left, if you're left-handed). Use a right angle to align the ruler, as in Figure 3 on page 20. Slice off uneven ends as in Figure 4, page 20, then proceed to cut at desired widths, running the cutter away from your body (Figure 5, page 20).

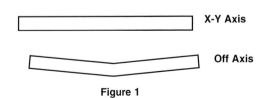

Figure 1

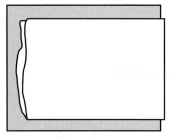

Figure 2

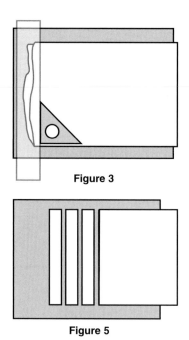

Figure 3

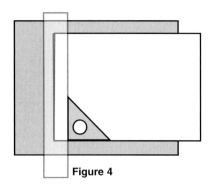

Figure 4

Figure 5

Muttonhead Tips for Safe and Successful Rotary Cutting

◆ Work on a firm, flat surface with plenty of elbowroom.

◆ Always run the cutter away from your body.

◆ Make a practice of setting the safety latch on the cutter every time you set it down. Some cutters have automatic safety mechanisms and this isn't a concern, but many require an extra step to set the safety latch. For the welfare of children, pets, and yourself, set the safety latch.

◆ Many self-healing mats have grids. Use the grid to align

the fold of the fabric. This helps keep slices on the true cross-grain.

◆ Few fabrics, such as stripes, plaids, or checks are printed on the true grain and cross-grain axes. You'll have to choose between strips with these prints on the cross-grain and strips with the prints running parallel to the cut end. For our purposes, we go with the print, rather than the cross-grain and use shorter strips to prevent distortion.

◆ When slicing many different fabrics in different-width strips, arrange strips on a folding drying rack placed next to the sewing machine. This makes it easy to select the print and width you want for the next placement.

Cutting Strips

All seam allowances in this book are 1/4", unless otherwise stated.

Inaccurate seam allowances can cause havoc with pieced blocks and borders. Check the accuracy of your 1/4" seam allowance with a piece of paper. Draw a line on the paper 1/4" away from the edge and running parallel to the edge. With the pressure foot up, insert the paper under the foot and pierce the paper with the needle (unthreaded). Lower the pressure foot to secure the paper; place a small piece of tape along the throat plate as a guide to a perfect 1/4" seam allowance.

Careful!

There are magnetic seam allowance guides available, but they should not be used with computerized sewing machines. The magnet can corrupt or erase information recorded in the computer unit.

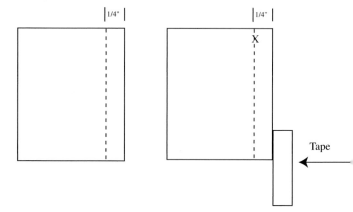

Preparing for Appliqué

Preparation for appliqué motifs, regardless of their size, is essentially the same. We've cut the background and border fabrics, and have chosen which prints will be used, and where. It's now time to bond the fusible web to the wrong side of the appliqué scraps.

Cut a piece of paper-backed fusible web slightly larger than the size of the appliqué piece, allowing at least 1/4" all around. Place the webbing on the wrong side of the fabric, with the adhesive side touching the fabric. Apply a pre-heated iron for the recommended time to create a minimum bond between the adhesive and the fabric.

Why, in the instructions, do we say "following manufacturer's directions," rather than spelling them out? Because each product is formulated a little differently and may have different requirements for successful use.

Place the pattern on the bonded fabric with the printed side of the pattern touching the paper backing. This ensures the pieces will be oriented the way they appear on the quilt.

If the design requires some patterns be cut reversed, use a marker to write "reversed" on the back side of the pattern. Then, place the pattern on the paper side with the word "reversed" touching the paper.

Trace the pattern with a pen or pencil. Cut it out with scissors. Cut out all pieces before removing any paper backing.

Position the appliqué pieces on the background fabric, referring to the photo and layout diagram for suggested color placement. When you are pleased with the arrangement, fuse the pieces in place with an iron, again following manufacturer's directions.

To hold the fabrics in place while working satin stitches around each shape and to prevent puckering in curves and corners, secure an iron-on, peel-off stabilizer on the wrong side of the background fabric underneath appliqué shapes.

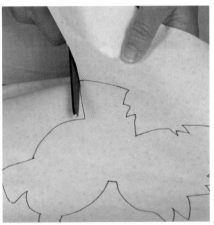
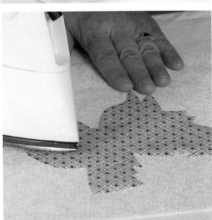
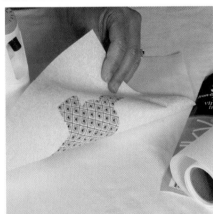

 Muttonhead Tips for Successful Appliqué

◆ In general, we use narrow satin stitches for features and details and a medium to medium-wide satin stitch to outline the shape.

◆ Rayon thread in the upper machine and coordinating all-purpose thread in the bobbin gives a nice, soft sheen to the satin stitches and precludes having to loosen the thread tension (nearly impossible on automatic tension machines).

Strip-Piecing around a Block

Basic, log-cabin strip-piecing is pretty straightforward, but we sometimes use a set-on method that results in a block without an obvious beginning and ending strip order, such as **Tiptoe Scotties** on page 58.

Instructions

1 Stitch a strip along one side of the center block, with a piece of the strip extending past the block equal to the cut width of the strip. So, if the strip is cut 2" wide, the strip would extend beyond the block 2", as in Figure 1.

2 Stitch strip #2 along side #2 of the center block, trimming it even with the edge of the block, as in Figure 2.

3 Strip #3 is stitched along side #3, trimming it even with the edge of the block, as in Figure 3.

4 Fold strip #1 up, out of the needle's path, as in Figure 4. Strip #4 is stitched along side #4, but stitching stops 1/4" away from the block's edge, as in Figure #5. Strip #4 is cut even with the edge of the block, as in Figure 6.

5 Fold strip #1 on the block, with right sides facing. The final portion of the seam is stitched, as in Figure 7. The finished block looks like Figure 8, with no obvious first or last strip.

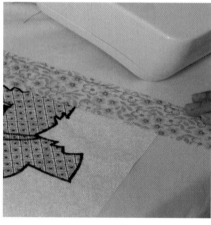

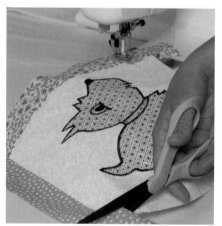

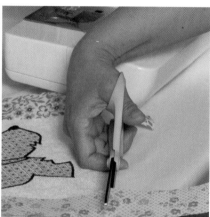

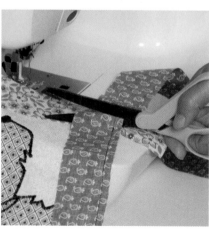

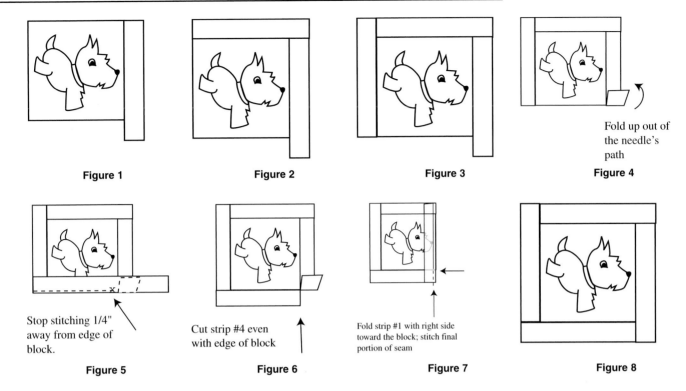

Figure 1

Figure 2

Figure 3

Fold up out of
the needle's
path

Figure 4

Stop stitching 1/4"
away from edge of
block.

Figure 5

Cut strip #4 even
with edge of block

Figure 6

Fold strip #1 with right side
toward the block; stitch final
portion of seam

Figure 7

Figure 8

Eyes

The eyes on a stylized animal or human character are very important. They, along with the eyebrows (if there are any), set the mood of the character. However, they can involve pretty tiny pieces, especially in a block design.

Instructions

1 We sometimes use small pieces of fabric, and we sometimes use a series of spiraling stitches.

2 Begin by outlining the eye with an arch of narrow zigzag stitches worked close together — but not quite satin stitching.

3 Then, stitch rounds of zigzag stitches, overlapping slightly. We finished the Scotty with an underline to suggest chubby cheeks.

Making a Quilt Sandwich

Instructions

1 Place backing fabric face down on the work surface. If you need to baste, tape the corners to the work surface with masking tape.

2 Unroll the batting, smoothing and patting to distribute evenly on the backing.

3 Center the quilt top on the backing/batting, allowing a small margin all around for take-up by quilting.

4 Baste or fuse layers together.

Binding

Muttonhead Sandy introduced us to a quick-and-easy method of binding quilts that we now use as a standard technique. This isn't a method you'd want to use on an heirloom quilt or one for competition, but for these colorful quilts, which will endure the rigors of being loved, used, and abused, this is a quick, attractive, and durable finish.

Instructions

1 Cut 2-1/2"-wide strips of binding fabric on the straight of the grain, or the bias. Join along short ends on an angle to create one long strip, as in Figures 1 and 2.

2 Press in half lengthwise, with wrong sides together, as in Figure 3.

3 Position folded strip along edge of quilt, with raw edges even. Stitch with a 3/8" seam allowance. Stop stitching 3/8" from the edge of the quit, as in Figure 4. Backstitch and snip threads.

5 Begin quilting from the center out to work any fullness toward the periphery. Quilt the grid along seam allowances, if yours is a block design, or quilt around center panel of a large-format quilt.

6 Quilt in the ditch or 1/4" away from seams for a tidy look, and to distribute and secure batting, before moving on to quilt around shapes.

7 Quilt inner, and then outer, borders.

8 Quilt around shapes, using echo quilting (concentric trips around each shape) if desired, for texture and durability.

4 Pivot the quilt. Fold binding straight up and align raw edges of binding with side #2 of the quilt.

5 Fold binding straight down, creating a small fold (Figure 6).

6 Insert the machine needle through the fold, 3/8" away from side #2 of the quilt corner. Backstitch; stitch to 3/8" of the next corner; repeat on all four corners.

7 Wrap fold of strip to back of quilt with fold slightly underlapping the binding seam on the front and encasing raw edges, as in Figure 7. Pin in place from the right side.

8 Stitch in the ditch from the right side of the quilt through all layers, securing the folded edge of binding to the wrong side and pivoting at corners, as in Figure 8.

Step 3

Step 4

Step 5

Step 6

Step 7

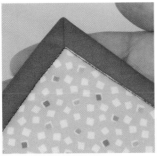

Step 8

Step 9

The finished binding looks like this from the back. We've used black thread to make it easy to see the stitching. You would use a coordinating thread, of course, to make stitching blend with the fabric.

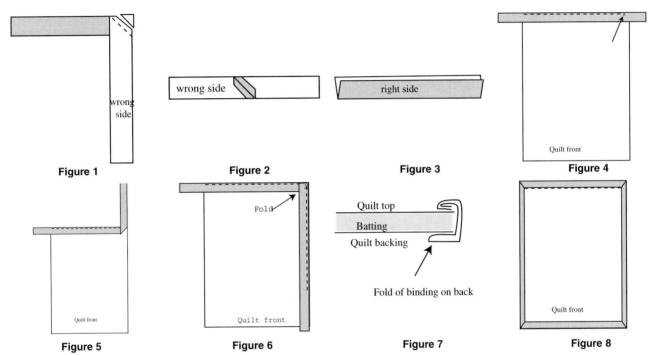

Figure 1

wrong side

Figure 2

right side

Figure 3

Quilt front

Figure 4

Quilt front

Figure 5

Fold

Quilt front

Figure 6

Quilt top

Batting

Quilt backing

Fold of binding on back

Figure 7

Quilt front

Figure 8

Enlarging or Reducing the Size of a Quilt

Sometimes, you just love a motif, but want a quilt larger or smaller than the project pictured. We know how you feel, and frequently adjust the size or complexity to fit a need or time limit. Feel free to use any of the following suggestions on any quilt in this book.

Muttonhead Tips to Enlarge a Repeated Block Design (including Scribble Quilts)

- ◆ Add additional rows and/or columns of blocks
- ◆ Add sashing
- ◆ Increase size of sashing
- ◆ Add strip-piecing

- ◆ Increase size of strips used
- ◆ Increase number of rounds of strip-piecing
- ◆ Make blocks larger and increase size of motif
- ◆ Add borders
- ◆ Increase size of borders
- ◆ Increase number of borders

To Enlarge a Large-Format Appliqué:

◆ Enlarge pattern pieces in center

◆ Enlarge center panel

◆ Add borders

◆ Increase size of borders

To reduce a Scribble Quilt:

◆ Reduce size of columns or blocks

◆ Reduce number of columns or blocks

◆ Reduce size of borders

To Reduce a Repeated Block Design (including a Scribble Quilt design)

◆ Reduce number of block rows and/or columns

◆ Remove sashing, if it's already in the design

◆ Reduce size of sashing

◆ Reduce size of strips used

◆ Make block smaller and reduce size of motif

◆ Make outer and inner borders smaller

Why isn't my quilt exactly the size on the layout diagram?

◆ Inaccurate seam allowances could be one reason. All seam allowances are 1/4", unless otherwise stated.

◆ How big is your batting? The thicker the batting, the more it will affect the size of the quilt.

◆ Have you applied a lot of quilting? The more quilting applied to the surface, the more it sucks up the width and length of the quilt.

To Reduce a Large-Format Appliqué:

◆ Reduce pattern pieces for center composition

◆ Reduce size of center panel

◆ Reduce size of borders

Increasing or Decreasing Complexity

Our goal is to share a variety of quilts for different skill levels and time budgets. Please feel free to use a simplified border for a quicker project, or add a border with more-involved piecing. Just remember to adjust the fabric requirements, backing, and batting needed to complete the quilt, and expectations on time.

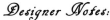Applique Block Quilts

Designer Notes:

Use 1/4" seam allowance throughout, unless otherwise stated.
Use all-purpose thread in machine top and bobbin for construction.
Use rayon thread in machine top and all-purpose thread in the bobbin for satin stitches.
Use rotary cutter, ruler, and self-healing mat to cut all strips and blocks.

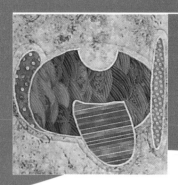

Littlest Prop Plane

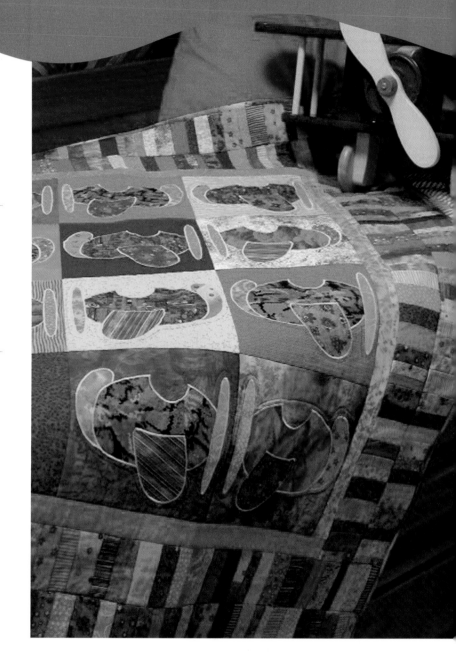

Finished size: 45" x 55"

Fabric Materials

12 (10-1/2") squares of fabrics that "read" as solids (see page 16)
3 or 4 brightly-colored prints (plane bodies)
Blue prints (wings)
Orange prints (propellers and inner borders)
Pink or fuchsia prints (tails)
48" x 58" piece of one fabric (backing)
1/2 yard of one fabric (binding)

Other Materials

48" x 58" piece quilt batting
Thread:
 Yellow rayon
 Yellow all-purpose
 Blue all-purpose (for construction)
Paper-backed fusible web
Iron-on, tear-away stabilizer

Designer Notes:

One plane popping out of its block adds to the cute factor and motion.
This adorable airplane is an adaptation of a quilt pattern found in an old book of quilt patterns. It was an outline of a realistic-looking warplane — not very cute for a baby quilt. To gain points on the cute scale, we rounded the edges, made it a side view, and shortened it for a pudgy plane any mom would want for her little one!

The original looked something like this.

The Muttonhead version looks like this.

Up, up, and away in adorable, brightly-colored, pudgy, prop planes. Alert snugglers can count the strips of fabric in the borders, while the planes can carry sleepyheads to a dreamland full of sunny skies!

Instructions

1 Cut 12 (10-1/2") squares from background fabrics.

2 Bond fusible web to wrong side of appliqué fabrics, following manufacturer's directions.

3 Place patterns on paper side of bonded fabrics with printing on patterns toward the paper backing. Trace 12 planes, wings, tails, and propellers (reversing six of each). Cut out with scissors; remove paper backing.

4 Position pieces on 11 squares, referring to layout diagram and photo for suggested placement. Bond in place with iron. Set one plane aside.

5 Secure stabilizer to wrong side of background squares, following manufacturer's directions.

6 Stitch around each appliqué shape with a medium satin stitch worked with rayon thread in the machine top and all-purpose thread in the bobbin.

7 Remove stabilizer; press each square thoroughly.

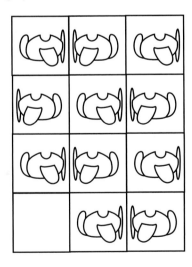

Figure 1

8 Stitch blocks together in rows and rows together to create a center panel, as in Figure 1. Press.

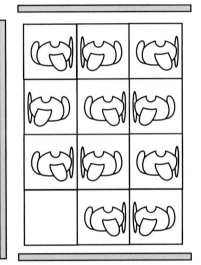

Figure 2

9 Cut four 2"-wide strips of orange prints for inner border. Stitch one strip along each side, top, and bottom of center panel (Figure 2), trimming strips even with the center panel edge. Press seam allowances toward the borders.

10 Cut strips of remaining fabrics in varying widths (1-1/4", 1-1/2", 1-3/4", and 2") and at least 14" long.

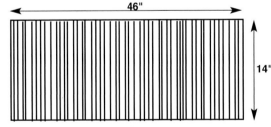

Figure 3

11 Stitch together along long edges to create four sheets of construction at least 46" long, as in Figure 3. Press seam allowances all in the same direction.

12 Cut four 3-1/2" x 43-1/2" strips for side outer borders and four 3-1/2" x 45-1/2" strips for top and bottom outer borders.

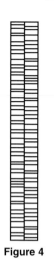

Figure 4

13 Stitch strips together in pairs, as in Figure 4.

14 Stitch side border strips in place, then top and bottom; press quilt top well.

15 Position reserved plane coming out of lower left block, referring to photo and layout diagram for placement. Bond. Satin-stitch.

16 Layer backing, batting, and quilt top. Baste through all layers to secure.

17 Quilt close to seam allowances in the center grid, then work toward outer edges. Quilt around each plane shape for definition and dimension.

18 Trim backing and batting even with quilt top. Press thoroughly.

19 Bind edges with 2-1/2"-wide strips, referring to Binding Technique on page 24.

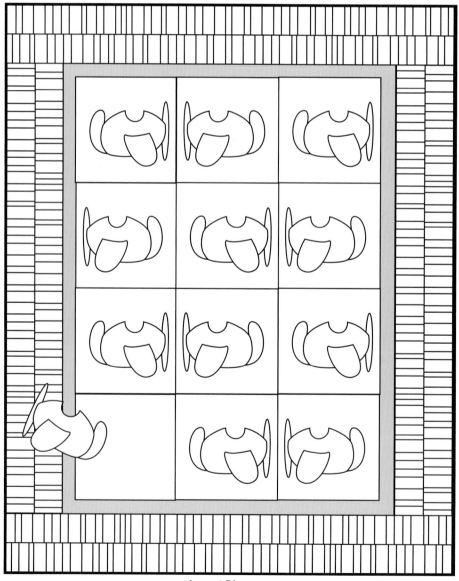

Layout Diagram

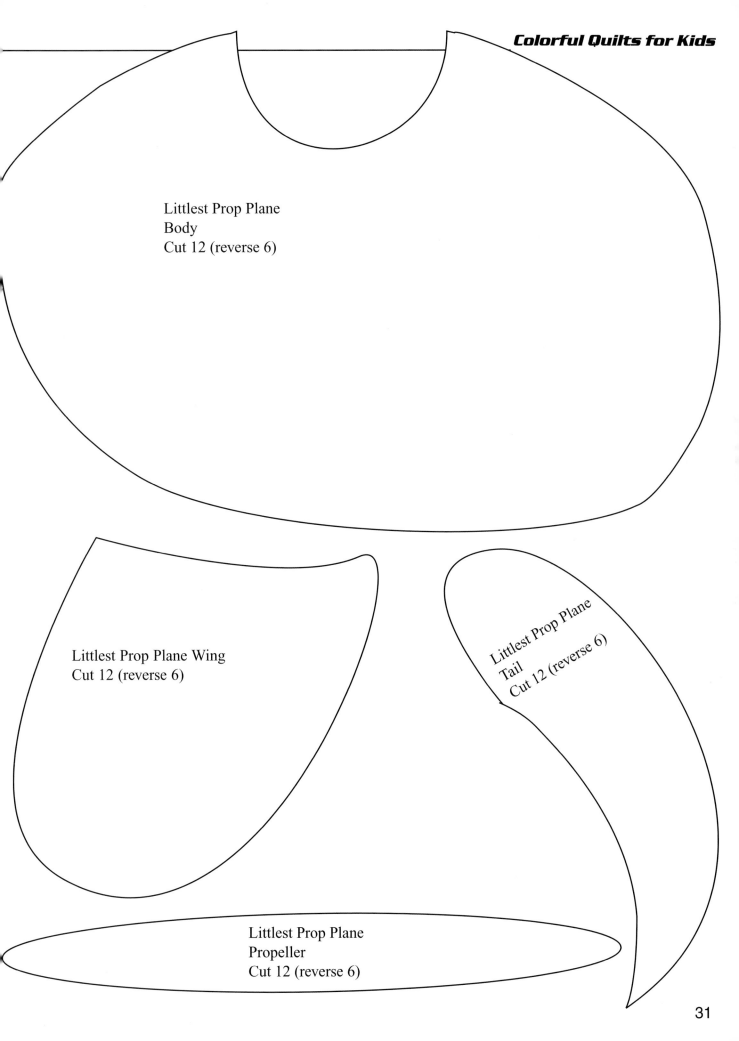

Littlest Prop Plane
Body
Cut 12 (reverse 6)

Littlest Prop Plane Wing
Cut 12 (reverse 6)

Littlest Prop Plane
Tail
Cut 12 (reverse 6)

Littlest Prop Plane
Propeller
Cut 12 (reverse 6)

Big-Mouth Frog

Finished size: 46" x 46"

Fabric Materials

Assorted bright prints (purple, pink, yellow, blue)
At least two yellow prints
4 or more pink or fuchsia prints
White scraps (eyes)
Assorted green prints (frog bodies)
49" x 49" piece of one fabric (backing)
1/2 yard one print (binding)

Other Materials

49" x 49" piece quilt batting
Thread:
 Green rayon
 Green all-purpose
 Black rayon
 Black all-purpose
 Bright pink all-purpose (for construction)
Paper-backed fusible web
Iron-on, tear-away stabilizer
Chalk pencil or fade-out pen

Designer Notes:

One way to increase placement on the cute scale is with bright colors and simple strip-piecing techniques around the block. Each block in the Big-Mouth Frog quilt has brightly-colored fabrics stitched around the square in simple log-cabin style.

Big-Mouth Frog was inspired by fabric in a photo of a child's playsuit from the 1930s. I added a tummy so rotund his mouth hangs over it.

Instructions

1 Cut eight 9-1/2" squares and one 10" x 9-1/2" blocks of fabric that "read" as solids (see page 16) for background blocks. Cut 1-1/2"-wide strip of each fabric for strip piecing, four 2"-wide strips of pink prints for inner border, and four 2-1/2"-wide strips of dark-value prints for outer border.

2 Bond fusible web to wrong side of appliqué fabrics, following manufacturer's directions.

3 Place patterns on paper side of bonded fabrics with print of pattern toward paper backing. Trace eight frog pieces; cut out with scissors. Remove paper backing.

4 Position pieces on background squares, referring to photo and layout diagram for placement. Fuse in place.

5 Secure stabilizer on wrong side of background blocks, following manufacturer's directions.

6 Draw features and details with chalk pencil.

7 Stitch around features and details with narrow satin stitches worked with black rayon thread in machine top and black all-purpose thread in bobbin. Outline frog with medium satin stitches worked in green rayon and all-purpose threads.

8 Remove stabilizer. Press blocks thoroughly.

This was originally intended as a Snuggle Quilt for a small boy ... but who could resist the temptation to present it to a student facing her first biology class!

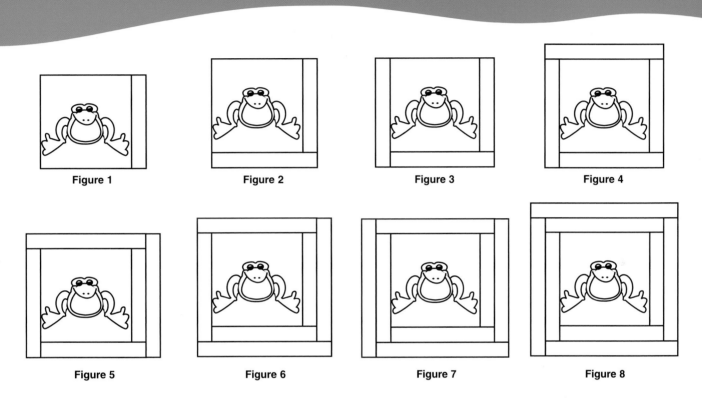

Figure 1   Figure 2   Figure 3   Figure 4

Figure 5   Figure 6   Figure 7   Figure 8

9 Stitch borders, log-cabin style, around each block, as in Figures 1–8.

10 Cut 10" x 9-1/2" block in half crosswise for two 5" x 9-1/2" blocks.

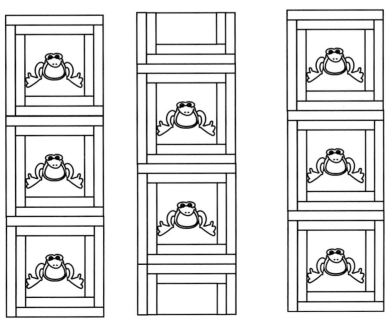

Figure 9

11 Arrange blocks and half blocks in rows, as in Figure 9 (page 33). Join rows to create center panel. Press seam allowances all in the same direction.

12 Stitch one inner border strip along each side of center panel, trimming each strip even with edge of center panel. Press seam allowances toward outer edges.

13 Stitch outer border strips along each side of center panel; press.

14 Layer backing, batting, and quilt top; baste through all layers to secure.

15 Quilt around each block, border seams, and frog, working from center to outer edge of quilt. Add other quilting, as desired.

16 Press thoroughly. Trim backing and batting even with quilt top.

17 Bind edges with 2-1/2"-wide strips, referring to Binding Technique on page 24.

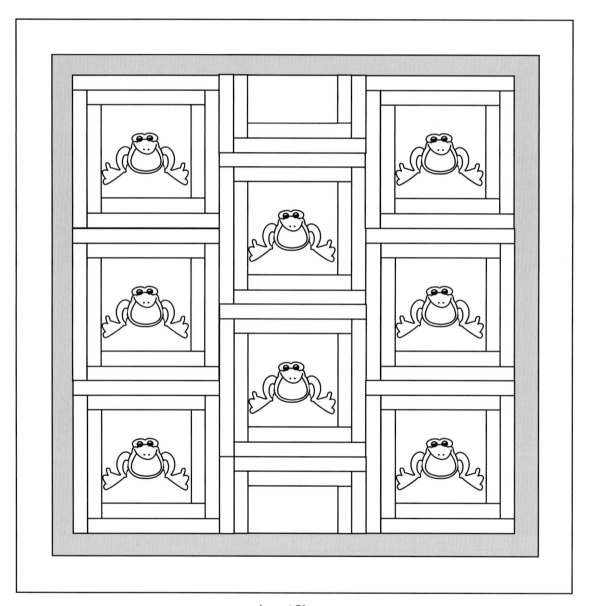

Layout Diagram

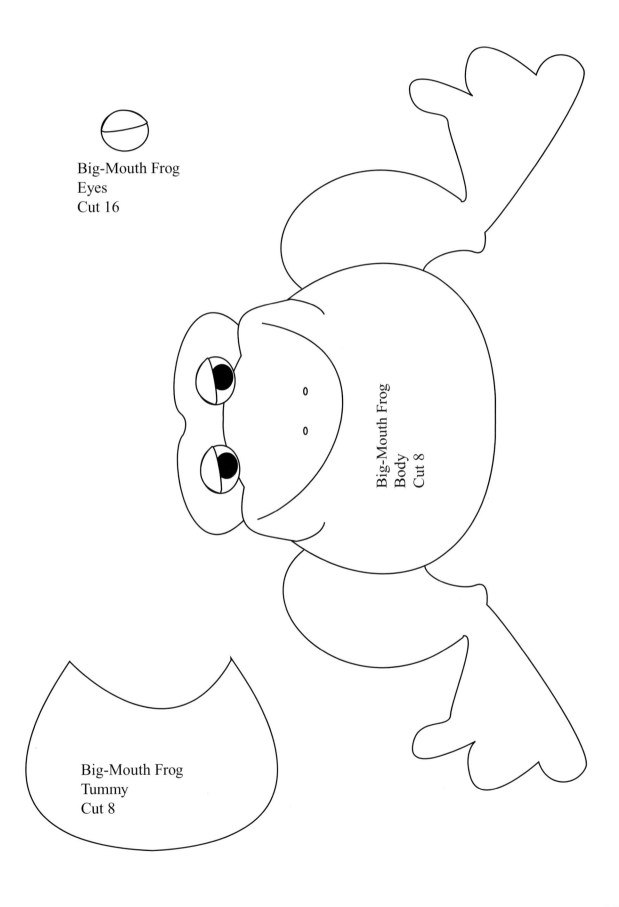

Big-Mouth Frog
Eyes
Cut 16

Big-Mouth Frog
Body
Cut 8

Big-Mouth Frog
Tummy
Cut 8

The Cat's Meow

Finished size: 42" x 42"

Fabric Materials

Assorted light-value lavender and pink prints (background blocks)

Assorted medium-value lavender prints (kitty faces and pieced border)

Assorted dark-value pink prints (tongues, kitty faces, pieced border)

Scraps of black (noses)

Scraps of white (eyes)

45" x 45" piece of fabric (backing)

1/2 yard of one fabric (binding)

Other Materials

45" x 45" piece quilt batting

Thread:
 Navy rayon
 Navy all-purpose
 Lavender rayon
 Lavender all-purpose

Paper-backed fusible web

Iron-on, tear-away stabilizer

Chalk pencil or fade-out pen

Designer Notes:

Kitty Cat appeared on a sheet of embroidery patterns with satin-stitched shading on her forehead. I turned that shaded area into a separate appliqué piece to use plenty of colorful scraps.

Note the position of the eyes; they make Kitty especially expressive.

If desired, pupils and noses may be embroidered with black thread or added with black fabric paints.

Instructions

1 Background blocks: From assorted light-value prints, cut five lavender 9-1/2" squares and four 9-1/2" pink squares for background blocks.

2 Bond fusible web on wrong side of appliqué fabrics, following manufacturer's directions.

3 Place patterns on paper side of bonded fabrics, print toward paper. Trace nine faces (reversing three), nine bangs (reversing three), nine

**The precious pussycats on this sweet topper
will delight any little miss!**

tongues, 18 eyes, 18 pupils, and nine noses. Cut out with scissors; remove paper backing.

4 Position pieces on background blocks, referring to photo and layout diagram. Fuse in place, following manufacturer's instructions.

5 Secure stabilizer on wrong side of each block, following manufacturer's instructions.

6 Draw facial details with tailor's chalk. Thread upper machine with navy rayon thread and bobbin with matching all-purpose thread. Set machine for narrow satin stitch, and stitch along chalk lines and around facial features.

7 Thread upper machine with purple rayon thread and bobbin with matching all-purpose thread. Set machine for medium satin stitch and stitch around kitty shapes.

8 Remove stabilizer. Press blocks thoroughly.

9 Referring to Layout Diagram, stitch blocks together in three rows of three, then stitch rows together to make the center panel. Press.

10 Inner border: From assorted medium-value lavender prints, cut four 2"-wide strips.

11 Attach border to center panel log-cabin style, stitching first strip across top of center panel, second strip down right side, third strip across bottom and fourth strip up left side, trimming strips even with center panel edge.

12 Outer border: From assorted fabrics, cut strips in varying widths: 1-1/4", 1-1/2", 1-3/4", 2", and 2-1/4". (If you're using up lots of scraps, each strip should be at least 7" long, and you'll make four sheets. If scraps are large enough, cut strips at least 24" along and make one sheet.)

13 Stitch strips together along long edges, alternating colors and widths, and offsetting each strip 1/2" as in Figure 1. Press all seam allowances in the same direction. Create a sheet at least 44" long.

14 Cut four 6-1/2" x 30-1/2" strips, as in Figure 2 (page 38).

15 Stitch strips together along long edges with ends even to create a sheet, as in Figure 3 (page 38). Cut four 6-1/2" squares from it, as in Figure 4 (page 38).

16 Arrange squares and strips, as in Figure 5 (page 38). Stitch together to create the quilt top. Press thoroughly.

17 Layer backing, batting, and quilt top; baste through all layers.

18 Quilt along the grid of seams (in the ditch, or 1/4" away from seam allowances) working center, inner border, then outer border. Quilt around each shape, including features if desired, for dimension.

19 Remove basting; press well. Trim backing and batting even with quilt top.

20. Bind edges using 2-1/2"-wide strips of one fabric used for bodies, referring to Binding Technique on page 24.

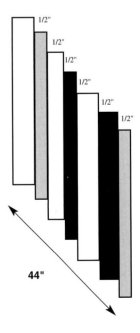

Figure 1

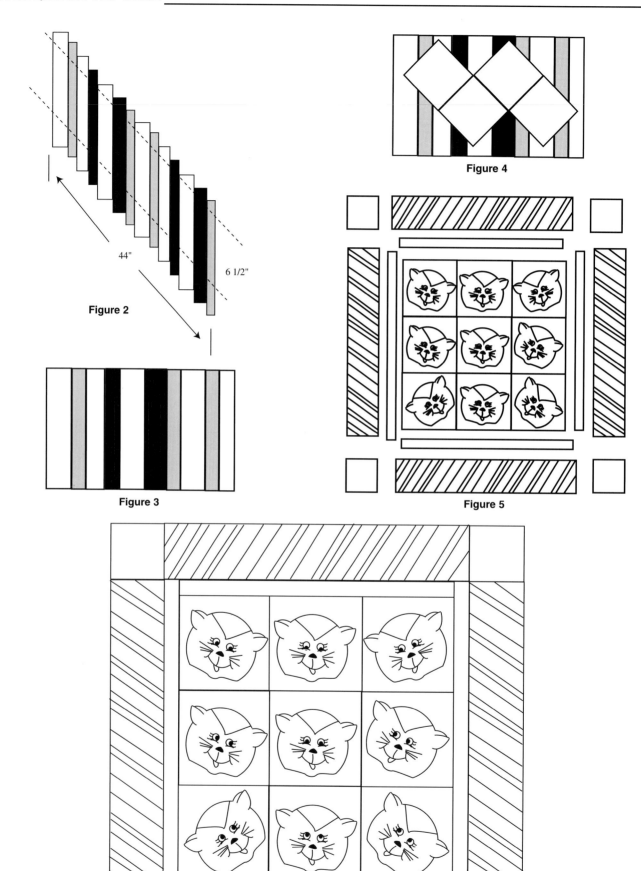

Figure 2

Figure 3

Figure 4

Figure 5

44"

6 1/2"

Layout Diagram

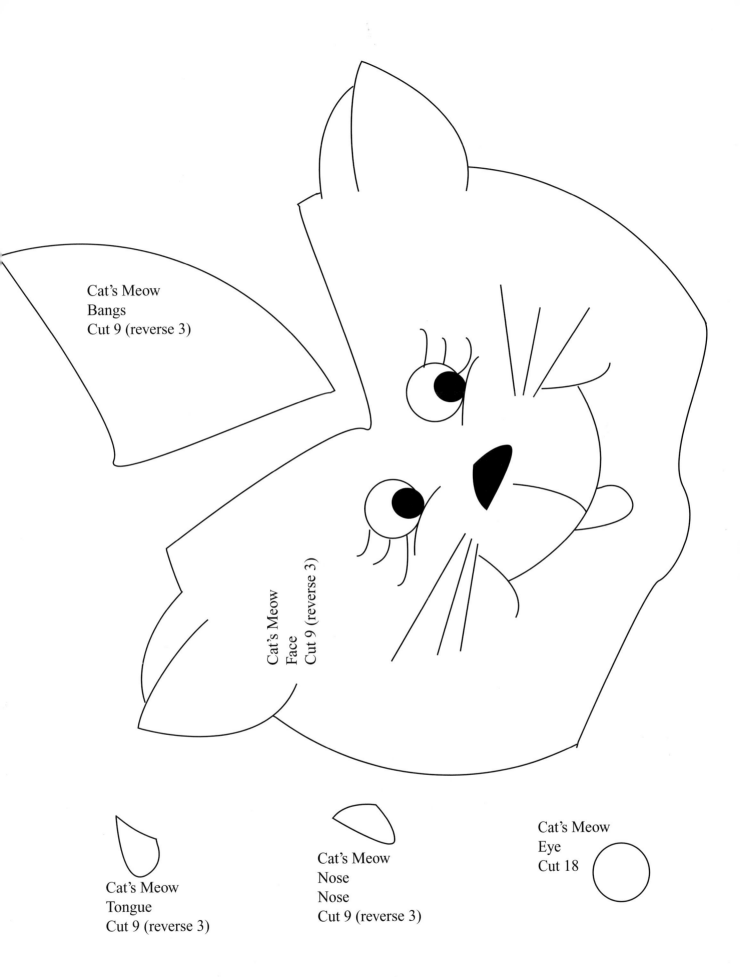

Cat's Meow
Bangs
Cut 9 (reverse 3)

Cat's Meow
Face
Cut 9 (reverse 3)

Cat's Meow
Tongue
Cut 9 (reverse 3)

Cat's Meow
Nose
Nose
Cut 9 (reverse 3)

Cat's Meow
Eye
Cut 18

39

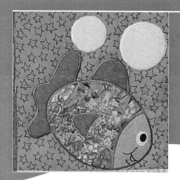

Fish Out of School

Finished size: 44" x 44"

Fabric Materials

Assorted light- and medium-value aqua prints (background blocks)

Assorted bright prints (fish)

Assorted bright prints that "read" as solids (face, fins, and tails)

White-on-white prints (bubbles)

1/2 yard dark-value, multi-colored print (inner border and fish pieces)

1/2 yard of four different aqua prints (outer border and fish pieces)

47" x 47" piece of one fabric (backing)

1/2 yard of one fabric (binding)

Other Materials

47" x 47" piece quilt batting

Thread:
 Aqua all-purpose
 Aqua rayon
 White all-purpose
 White rayon

Paper-backed fusible web

Iron-on, tear-away stabilizer

Chalk pencil or fade-out pen

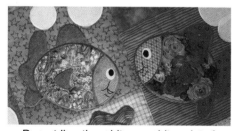

Do not line the white-on-white prints for air bubbles. For once, we want the background to "ghost" through the print to create the illusion of transparency.

Designer Notes:

Fish Out of School began as a single fish embroidered on a fingertip towel of an undetermined age. The direction of the bubbles caught my attention and resulted in the interesting placement of the fish. Regardless of the direction the fish face, the bubbles rise in the same direction.

The position of the two face-to-face fishes creates interesting interaction and a break from the usual block arrangement.

As a little girl, my dad and I would occasionally go fishing. I don't remember catching anything, but I cherish the memory of tromping through the warm grass with a fishing pole in one hand and a can of worms in the other — and the sound of Dad whistling as we made our way toward the water.

Instructions

1. Seven 10-1/2" squares and two 10-1/2" x 11" blocks of aqua print for background blocks.

2. Bond fusible web on wrong side of appliqué fabrics, following manufacturer's directions.

3. Place patterns on paper side of bonded fabrics with printing on patterns toward the paper backing. Trace nine bodies, tails, fins, and faces on paper side of bonded fabrics. Trace at least 18 bubbles (small and medium) on white prints. Cut all pieces out with scissors; remove paper backing.

4. Position pieces on blocks, referring to layout diagram for suggested placement. Note: Fish are not all positioned in center of blocks. Some are below the center line, some above, and some are placed diagonally on the block, creating variety, interest, and motion.

5. Bond pieces in place, following manufacturer's directions.

6. Secure stabilizer to wrong side of each block.

7. Draw facial features with chalk pencil or fade-out pen. Stitch along lines with narrow satin stitch worked in aqua rayon thread in the machine top and aqua all-purpose thread in the bobbin.

8. Stitch around fin, tail, and jaw line with medium satin stitch. Stitch around each body. Stitch around each air bubble with medium satin stitch worked in white threads.

9. Remove stabilizer. Press each block thoroughly.

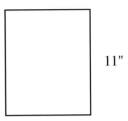

11"

10 1/2"

Figure 1

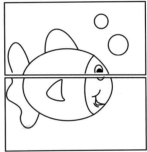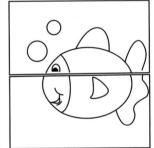

Figure 2

10. Cut the two 10-1/2" x 11" blocks in half to make four 10-1/2" x 5-1/2" blocks, as in Figures 1 and 2.

41

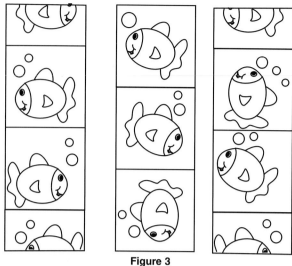

Figure 3

11 Arrange half blocks and blocks, as in Figure 3. Stitch blocks together into columns; stitch columns together into center panel. Press seam allowances all in the same direction.

12 Cut four 2-1/2"-wide strips from multi-colored print. Stitch one strip along each side of center panel, trimming excess border strip even with center panel. Press seam allowances toward border.

13 Cut four 5-1/2"-wide strips from aqua prints. Stitch one strip along each side; trim. Press.

14 Trace large bubbles in outer border with chalk pencil.

15 Layer backing, batting, and quilt top; baste through all layers to hold securely.

16 Working from center to perimeter, quilt along seam lines, around each fish shape, and air bubbles. Quilt outer air bubbles.

17 Remove basting. Press entire quilt thoroughly. Trim backing and batting even with quilt top.

18 Bind edges with 2-1/2"-wide strips of one fabric, referring to Binding Technique on page 24. Press thoroughly.

Layout Diagram

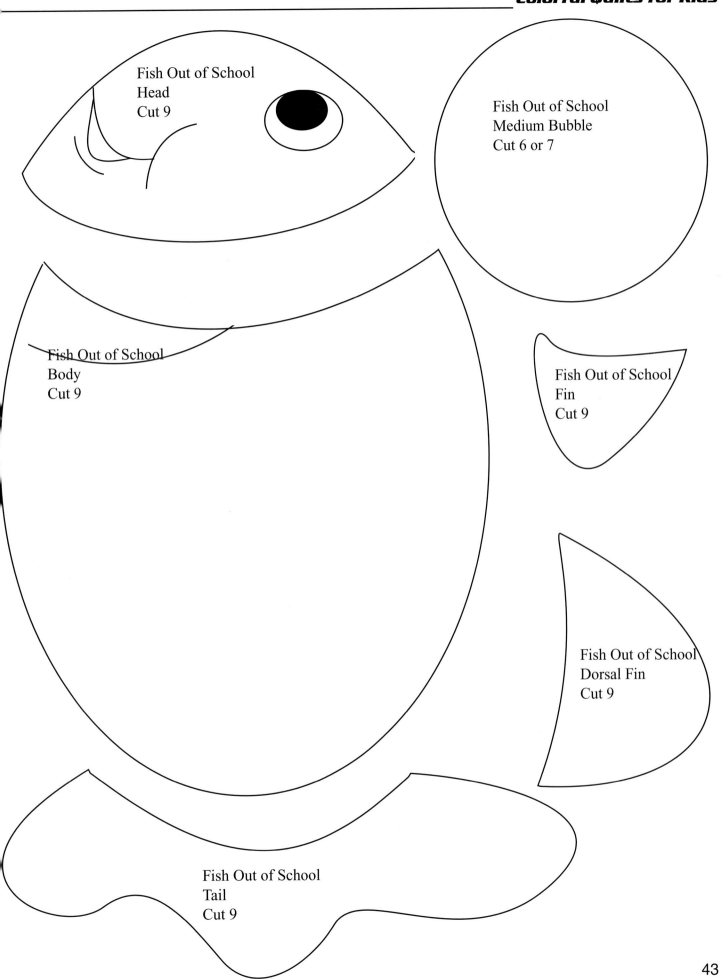

Fish Out of School
Head
Cut 9

Fish Out of School
Medium Bubble
Cut 6 or 7

Fish Out of School
Body
Cut 9

Fish Out of School
Fin
Cut 9

Fish Out of School
Dorsal Fin
Cut 9

Fish Out of School
Tail
Cut 9

Peek-A-Boo Bunny

Finished size: 53" x 53"

Fabric Materials

Assorted light-value yellow prints (background blocks)

Assorted light-value pink prints (bunny heads and outer ears)

Assorted dark-value pink prints (inner ears, noses, and inner border)

Scraps of black for pupils (or black fabric paint)

Scraps of white (eyes and teeth)

At least four assorted medium-value pink prints (block borders)

56" x 56" piece of one fabric (or constructed fabrics for backing)

Other Materials

56" x 56" piece quilt batting
Thread:
 Black rayon
 Black all-purpose
 Pink rayon
 Pink all-purpose
Paper-backed fusible web
Iron-on, peel-off stabilizer
Tailor's chalk

Designer Notes:

    There's a lot going on in this deceptively simple, repeated-motif composition. We used a partial motif in the center block and a single row of sashing around each square. Simple changes can make a big difference in the cute factor of a quilt.

    Peek-A-Boo Bunny was all alone when I found her in an iron-on transfer pattern from the '40s. I isolated her face, because that's where the action was — and to increase the size of pieces. It's no fun to work on an appliqué project when the pieces are too small.

One little sweetie in the center is a little on the shy side — but the rest of these bunnies can't wait to hop across this fun quilt. It's a perfect choice for your own snuggle bunny!

Instructions

1 Background blocks: From assorted light-value yellow prints, cut nine 10-1/2" squares for background blocks.

2 Bunnies: Bond fusible web to backs of fabrics for bunnies. Place patterns on paper side of bonded fabrics, print toward paper. For each of the nine bunnies, trace one head from a light-value pink; two outer ears (reversing one) from a second light-value pink; two inner ears (reversing one) and a nose from dark-value pinks; one set teeth and two eyes (reversing one) from white. Cut out with scissors; peel off paper backing.

3 Position bunny heads, ears, inner ears, eyes, noses, and teeth on background blocks, referring to photo and Layout Diagram, and positioning bunny for center block off edge of background block. Fuse in place following manufacturer's instructions.

4 Secure stabilizer behind appliqués, following manufacturer's instructions.

5 Draw facial details with tailor's chalk. Work eyes with black rayon thread in machine top and black all-purpose thread in bobbin, referring to Spiral technique on page 23. Stitch along remaining chalk lines with narrow satin stitches worked with pink rayon thread in machine top and pink all-purpose thread in bobbin.

6 With machine set for short, medium-wide, satin stitch, stitch around all components of bunnies and over detail lines. Remove stabilizer. Press blocks thoroughly.

7 Block borders: From assorted, medium-value, pink prints, cut 36 (2-1/2"-wide) strips at least 13" long.

8 Stitch strips around each block, referring to the Tiptoe Scottie sashing technique on page 22.

9 Referring to Layout Diagram, sew bunny blocks together in rows of three, then sew rows together to make center panel.

10 Inner border: Cut assorted dark-value pink prints into strips 3" wide and of varying lengths; sew together end to end, alternating lengths, to make four strips at least 48" long. Stitch strips to edges of bunny panel, trimming ends even.

11 Outer border: Cut fabrics of assorted colors and values into strips 3-1/2" wide and of varying lengths; sew together end to end, alternating lengths, to make four strips at least 54" long. Stitch strips to edges of quilt, staggering positions of seam lines and trimming ends even.

12 Press thoroughly, pressing seam allowances toward outside.

13 Layer backing, batting, and quilt top; baste through all layers.

14 Stitch along the block grid, working from center to periphery. Quilt in the ditch or 1/4" away from seam, as desired. Quilt around each shape as desired.

15 Remove basting; press well. Trim backing and batting even with quilt top.

16 Bind edges using 2-1/2"-wide strips of one fabric used for bodies, referring to Binding Technique on page 24.

Layout Diagram

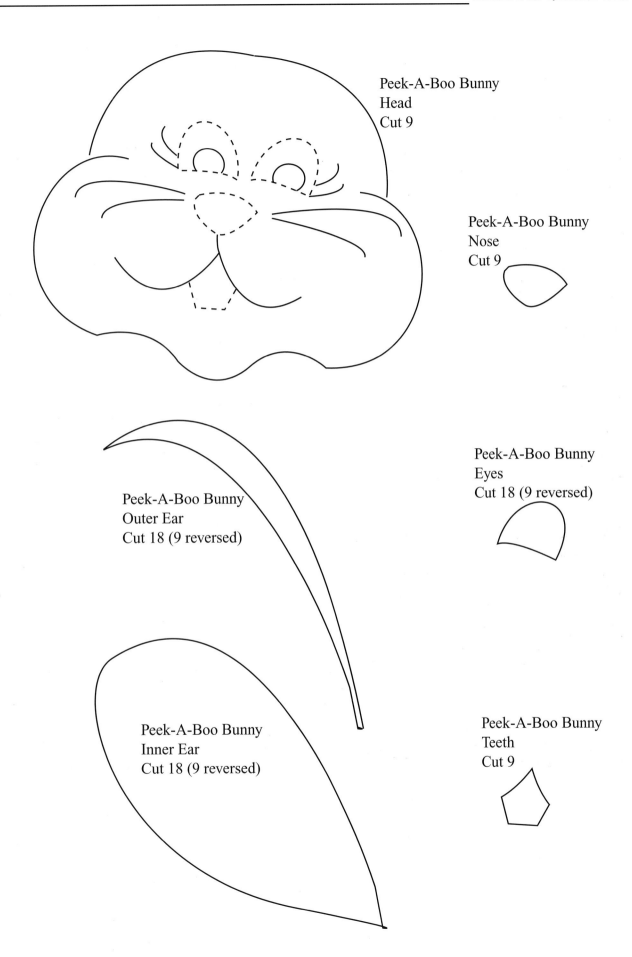

Peek-A-Boo Bunny
Head
Cut 9

Peek-A-Boo Bunny
Nose
Cut 9

Peek-A-Boo Bunny
Eyes
Cut 18 (9 reversed)

Peek-A-Boo Bunny
Outer Ear
Cut 18 (9 reversed)

Peek-A-Boo Bunny
Inner Ear
Cut 18 (9 reversed)

Peek-A-Boo Bunny
Teeth
Cut 9

Puppy Love

Finished size: 50" x 50"

Fabric Materials

Red prints: light-, medium-, and dark-value
Black prints: light-, medium-, and dark-value
Red-and-black prints: light- and dark-value
53" x 53" backing

Other Materials

53" x 53" piece quilt batting
Thread:
  Black rayon
  Black all-purpose
  Red rayon
  Red all-purpose
Paper-backed fusible web
Iron-on, peel-off stabilizer
Dinner plate
Tailor's chalk

Designer Notes:

The scalloped edge makes binding this quilt challenging. Feel free to stop at Step 16 and bind for a straight-edge quilt requiring less time; we just had to do it once!

This cutie appeared on the pocket of an embroidered apron from the late '40s. I added the curve of the ears and a perky tail for cute factor.

Instructions

1 Cut five 12-1/2" squares of light-value red prints for background, one 13-1/8" square for corner triangles, and two 13" squares for side triangles.

2 Cut square for corner triangles diagonally, as in Figure 1. Cut squares for side triangles in half diagonally, as in Figure 2.

3 Bond fusible web to wrong side of black and red prints for appliqué, following manufacturer's directions.

4 Place patterns on paper side of bonded fabrics with print on the patterns facing the paper backing. Trace five faces on light-value black prints, five lower ears on medium-value black prints, and five bodies, noses, and 10 pupils on dark-value black prints. Trace five ears, bangs, tongues, and upper ears on red prints. Cut out with scissors; remove paper backing.

5 Position puppy pieces on background blocks, referring to Layout Diagram and photo for suggested placement. Fuse pieces in place.

6 Secure stabilizer to back of each block, following manufacturer's directions.

7 Draw facial features with chalk pencil. Stitch along lines with a narrow zigzag stitch worked

**Red and black was a popular color combination
in vintage fabrics — printed and embroidered.
The friendly expression on the cute puppy faces
makes you just want to smile!**

with black rayon thread in the machine top and black all-purpose thread in the bobbin.

8 Stitch around tail, body, ears, and face (in that order) with a medium satin stitch.

9 Remove stabilizer; press blocks thoroughly.

10 Join corner triangles, side triangles, and appliqué blocks in rows, as in Figure 3 (page 50), noting the new position of the corner triangle points, as cut in Figure 1. Join rows into center panel. Press.

11 Cut four 2-1/2"-wide strips of dark-value red prints for inner border. Stitch one along each side of center panel, trimming as necessary. Press seam allowances toward border strips.

12. Cut remaining scraps into strips of various widths (1-1/4", 1-1/2", 1-3/4", 2") and at least 9" long.

13 Join strips along long edges, as in Figure 4 (page 50), varying colors and widths of strips. Make four sheets at least 55" long. Press seam allowances all in the same direction.

14 Trim uneven edges for a border strip 6-1/2" wide.

15 Stitch one border strip along each side of center panel, starting and stopping stitching 1/4" away from each edge, as in Figure 5 (page 50). Border should extend evenly beyond each edge of center panel 8-1/2" (width of border, plus 2"). Press border strip open. Repeat on all four corners, as in Figure 6 (page 50).

16 Fold quilt top diagonally, with edges even and draw a line from the corner to the end of the border at a 45 degree angle, as in Figure 7 (page 50). Stitch along with line and cut off excess, leaving 1/4" seam allowance. Open fold and press seam open. Corner should look like Figure 8 (page 50). Repeat for all four corners.

17 Place scallop pattern on one border with center of scallop pattern along center line of border. Trace scallop with chalk pencil. Repeat in each direction, working toward corner.

18 Place a dinner plate or saucer on one corner and trace the curve, stopping at the scallop chalk line, as in Figure 9 (page 50).

19 Layer backing, batting, and quilt top; baste through all layers to secure.

20 Quilt along seam lines (in the ditch or 1/4" away), working from quilt center to periphery. Quilt around shapes and features as desired for dimension.

21 Remove basting stitches. Press well.

22 Cut along scallop line through all layers.

23 Bind edges with 2-1/2"-wide strips of one fabric, pivoting at corners (refer to Binding Technique on page 24).

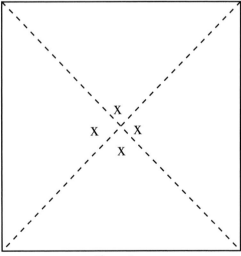

Figure 1

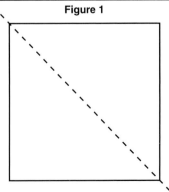

Figure 2

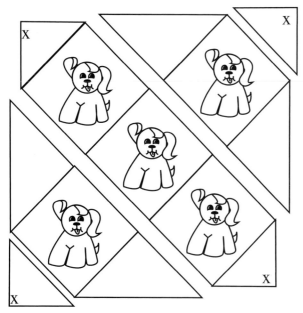

Figure 3

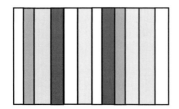

Figure 4

Start stitching here   Stop stitching here

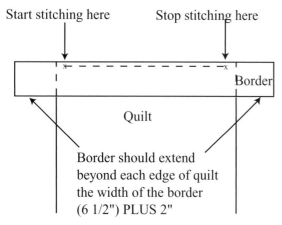

Border

Quilt

Border should extend
beyond each edge of quilt
the width of the border
(6 1/2") PLUS 2"

Figure 5

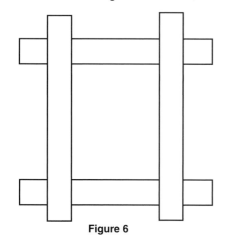

Figure 6

Stitching line

Cutting line
1/4" away

Remove excess.

Fold

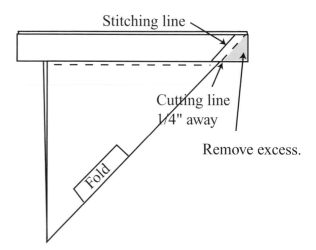

Figure 7

One corner
mitered

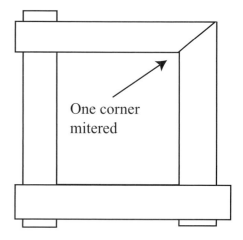

Figure 8

Join chalk lines

Dinner
plate

Figure 9

Layout Diagram

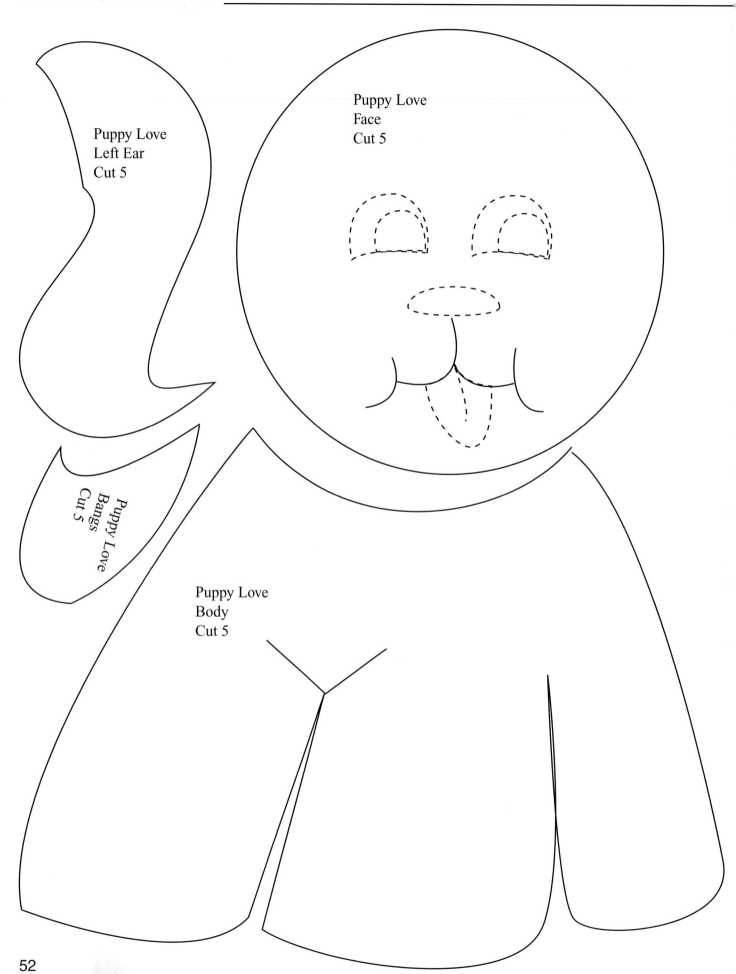

Puppy Love
Left Ear
Cut 5

Puppy Love
Face
Cut 5

Puppy Love
Bangs
Cut 5

Puppy Love
Body
Cut 5

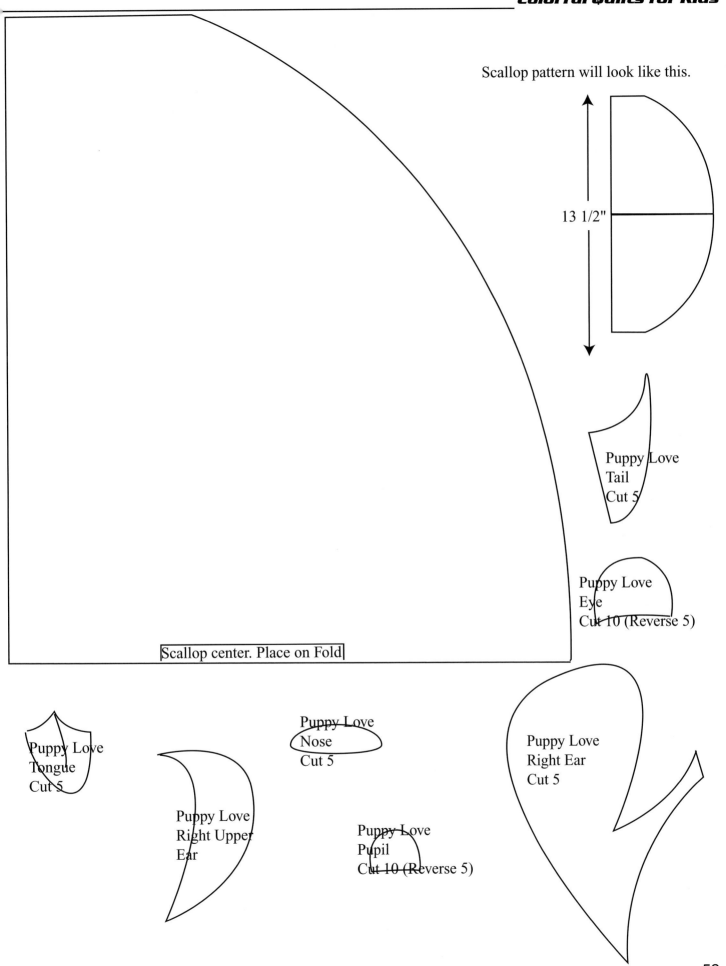

Scallop pattern will look like this.

13 1/2"

Puppy Love
Tail
Cut 5

Puppy Love
Eye
Cut 10 (Reverse 5)

Scallop center. Place on Fold

Puppy Love
Tongue
Cut 5

Puppy Love
Right Upper
Ear

Puppy Love
Nose
Cut 5

Puppy Love
Pupil
Cut 10 (Reverse 5)

Puppy Love
Right Ear
Cut 5

Sailboats in the Wind

Finished size: 48" x 57"

Materials

Assorted light-value red prints (inner blocks)
1 yard print (outer border strips) (or 1 yard
    red-and-white stripe for outer borders)
Pieces of at least three dark-value blue prints
    (blocks and boats)
Assorted light-value blue prints (sailboat back
    grounds)
Pieces of at least three dark-value red prints
    (corner blocks, boats, and inner borders)
3/8 yard print for binding
Assorted medium-value blue prints (corner
    blocks)
1/2 yard print (outer border strips) (or 1/2 yard
    red-and-blue print for outer border strips)
Remnant of white-on-white print (sails)
51" x 60" backing

Other Materials

51" x 60" piece quilt batting
Thread:
 Red rayon
 Red all-purpose
 Navy rayon
 Navy all-purpose
Paper-backed fusible web
Iron-on, peel-away stabilizer
Tailor's chalk

Designer Notes:

Is it possible to approach the same color combination with the same motif and make two quilts look different? That is the challenge on this and sister quilt (Sailboat in the Wind Scribble version) on page 118. The answer is "yes." Each quilt has its own charm and yet is very different.

White prints are deceptive! Often, they won't exhibit "ghosting" qualities until fused on the background block. To prevent "ghosting," line the sails with solid white cotton.

The sailboat was inspired by a motif appearing in the catalog of a company producing iron-on transfer patterns in the '30s, '40s, and '50s. I changed it so the curve made the back of the boat look like the blowing waves were lapping at it.

Scudding over the whitecaps of your little guy's bed, these cheerful sailboats bring a breezy, nautical air to the décor. It's lovely as a throw, too, in a sunroom or den decorated with lighthouses, buoys, sea birds, and other beach motifs.

Instructions

1 Inner nine-patch blocks: Cut 30 (3-1/2") squares from assorted dark-value blue prints and 24 (3-1/2") blocks from assorted light-value reds. Alternating blues and reds and positioning blue squares in corners, stitch squares into six, nine-patch blocks as shown in Figure 1.

2 Sailboat blocks: From assorted light-value blue prints, cut six 9-1/2" squares for background blocks.

3 Sailboats: Bond fusible web to backs of fabrics for boats and sails, following manufacturer's directions: three dark-value blues and three dark-value reds for boats, and white-on-white print for sails.

4 Place patterns on paper side of bonded fabrics, with print on patterns toward paper. Trace six sails on white-on-white print; trace a boat on each of three dark-value blues and three dark-value reds. Cut out with scissors; peel off paper backing.

5 Position sails and boats on light blue background blocks; fuse in place following manufacturer's instructions.

6 Iron stabilizer behind appliqués, following manufacturer's directions.

7 Draw sail details and masts with tailor's chalk. With machine set for narrow to medium satin stitch, stitch around sails and boats, and add detail and masts, using navy thread for navy boats and red thread for red boats. Trim away excess stabilizer.

8 Referring to Figure 3 on page 56, stitch nine-patch blocks and sailboat blocks together to make quilt center.

9 From assorted dark-value reds, cut four 2" strips for inner border; stitch one to each side of center panel, trimming ends of strip even with center panel. Press seam allowances toward borders.

10 Corner nine-patch blocks: Cut 20 (3-1/2") squares from assorted dark-value red prints and 16 (3-1/2") blocks from assorted medium-value blues. Alternating blues and reds and positioning red squares in corners, stitch squares into four, nine-patch blocks as in Step 1.

11 Outer border strips: From red-and-white striped or light-value red fabric, cut eight 3-1/2"-wide strips, four at least 32" long for top and bottom and four at least 41" long for sides; from medium-value blue or red-and-blue print, cut four 3-1/2"-wide strips, two at least 32" long and two at least 41" long. Sew a blue strip between two striped strips of the same length (Figure 2, page 56); repeat to make four border panels. Press seam allowances toward center strip.

12 Top and bottom borders: Sew a corner block to each end of one of the shorter border panels; repeat. See Figure 4, page 56.

13 Stitch side borders to quilt top; stitch top and bottom borders and corner blocks in place.

14 Layer backing, batting, and quilt top; baste through all layers.

15 Quilt in the ditch or 1/4" away from seams in the inner grid, working from center to periphery. Stitch along border seams. Quilt around sailboat shapes as desired for dimension.

16 Remove basting; press well. Trim backing and batting even with quilt top.

17 Bind edges with 2-1/2"-wide strips of one dark-value red print, referring to Binding Technique on page 24.

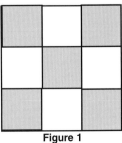

Figure 1

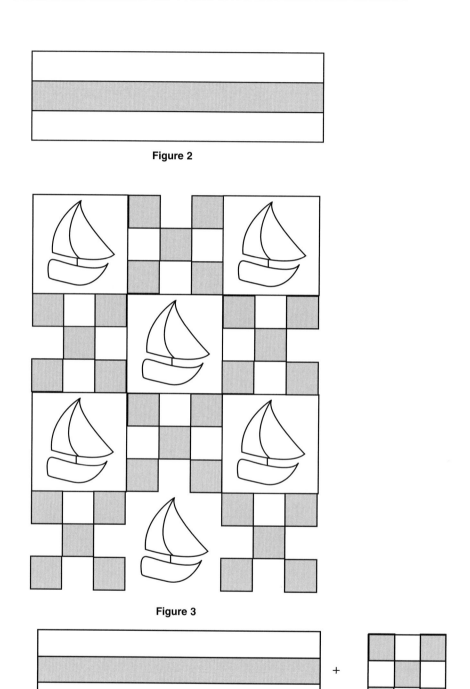

Figure 2

Figure 3

Figure 4

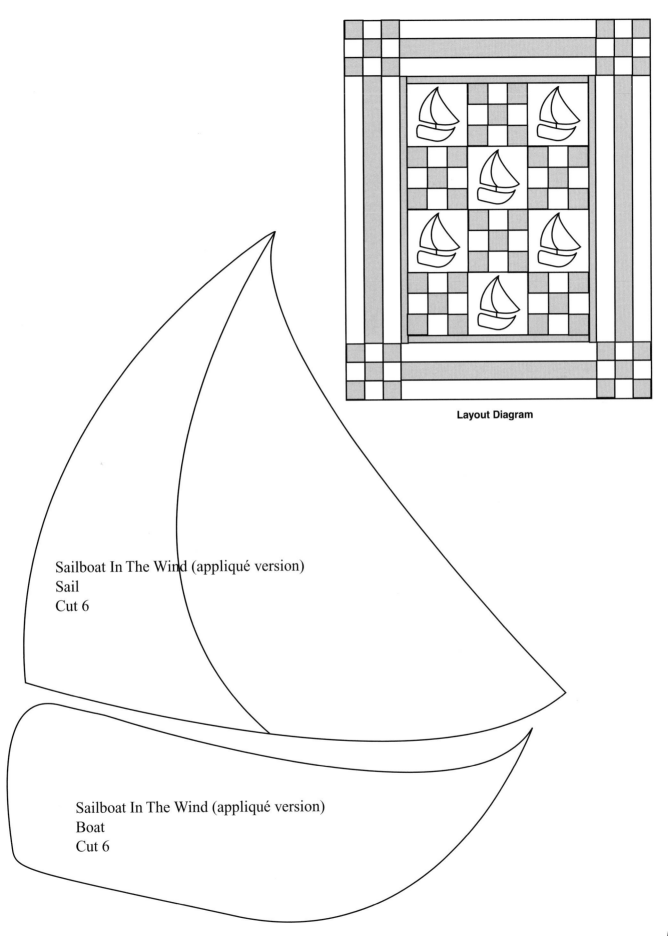

Layout Diagram

Sailboat In The Wind (appliqué version)
Sail
Cut 6

Sailboat In The Wind (appliqué version)
Boat
Cut 6

Tiptoe Scotties

Finished size: 45" x 45"

Fabric Materials

Cream-on-white prints (background blocks)
Vintage reproduction prints in desired colors
1/4 yard of four prints (inner borders)
1/2 yard of one print (outer border)
1/2 yard of one print (binding)
48" x 48" backing

Other Materials

48" x 48" piece quilt batting
Thread:
 Black rayon
 Black all-purpose
 Neutral all-purpose (for construction)
Paper-backed fusible web
Iron-on, peel-off stabilizer

Designer Notes:

We used vintage and reproduction fabrics and black threads to complete the retro look of this quilt. You might choose a blanket stitch for the appliqué outline, if your sewing machine offers this option.

The tiptoeing Scotty was on a sheet of iron-on transfers for children's clothing with no date on it. I loved the detail in his beard and added the kicking heels with a pudgy puppy tummy as a reminder of the way our Scotty, Kippy, ran when she was young.

Rather than making one block and slicing it in half for the half-blocks at the top and bottom of the center column, we placed the pattern on the block and satin-stitched half the Scotty shape in each half block.

How did Scotties become so popular — and remain popular for decades? Perky ears and tails might have something to do with their cute factor!

Instructions

1 Cut eight 9-1/2" squares and two 9-1/2" x 5" pieces of cream-on-white prints for background blocks. Cut 2"-wide strips of prints for sashing.

2 Bond fusible web to wrong side of 10" scraps for Scotties, following manufacturer's directions.

3 Place pattern on paper side of bonded fabric with print on pattern toward paper backing. Trace eight Scotties (reversing four); cut out with scissors. Remove paper backing.

4 Position Scotties on background blocks; fuse in place.

5 Secure stabilizer to wrong side of each block, including half blocks, following manufacturer's directions.

6 Stitch eyes and noses, referring to Spiral Technique on page 23 using narrow satin stitch worked with black rayon thread in machine top and black all-purpose thread in bobbin. Stitch collar with medium satin stitch. Stitch around each Scottie with a medium satin stitch.

7 Stitch the top half of one Scottie outline on one half block and the bottom half of one Scottie outline on the remaining half block.

8 Remove stabilizer. Press blocks thoroughly.

9 Stitch one strip of sashing along each side of Scottie blocks, referring to technique on page 22. Press seam allowances toward sashing.

10 Join blocks in columns and columns into a center panel, referring to Layout Diagram on page 60 for placement. Press thoroughly.

11 Cut 2-1/2"-wide strips of four medium-value prints for inner border and 3"-wide strips of one lighter-value print for outer border.

12 Stitch one 2-1/2"-wide strip along each side of center panel, trimming the strip even with edge of center panel.

13 Stitch one 3"-wide strip along each side of center panel, trimming strip even. Press thoroughly.

14 Layer backing, batting, and quilt top; baste through all layers to secure.

15 Quilt in the ditch or 1/4" away from seams joining blocks, working from center toward periphery. Quilt along all blocks, inner border, then outer border. Quilt around each Scotty and feature, as desired for dimension.

16 Remove basting; press thoroughly. Trim backing and batting even with quilt top.

17 Bind edges with 2-1/2"-wide strips, referring to Binding Technique on page 24.

Layout Diagram

Tiptoe Scotties
Body pattern
Cut 8 (3 reversed)

Finished size: 48" x 53"

Fabric Materials

Assorted light-value blue prints (background blocks)
1/3 yard striped blue fabric (corner squares)
Assorted yellow and orange prints (sashing)
Scraps of assorted print fabrics: blues and greens (wings and heads)
1 yard multicolor print (bodies and binding)
51" x 56" backing

Other Materials

51" x 56" piece quilt batting
Thread:
 Black rayon
 Black all-purpose
 Neutral all-purpose (construction)
Paper-backed fusible web
Iron-on, peel-off stabilizer
Chalk pencil or fade-out pen

Designer Note:

Rotating one block adds interest to a repeated-block design. Of course, the bright fabrics prevent any boredom through repetition!

There's always one that takes the path less traveled! In this case, it's the bug in the upper left corner — flying his own way over the colorful landscape of this happy throw!

Instructions

1 Background and sashing: From assorted light-value blue prints cut 12 (12-1/2") squares for background blocks. From blue striped fabric cut 20 (3-1/2") squares for corner blocks. From assorted orange and yellow fabrics, cut 31 (3-1/2" x 12-1/2") strips for sashing.

2 Dragonflies: Bond web to backs of fabrics for dragonflies: assorted blue and green prints for heads and wings, and multicolor print for bodies.

3 Place patterns on paper side of bonded fabrics, print toward paper. For each of the 12 dragonflies, trace one head from a blue or green print; a pair of upper wings, reversing one, from a second blue or green print; a pair of lower wings, reversing one, from a third blue or green print; and one body from multicolored print. Cut out with scissors; peel off paper backing.

4 Position dragonflies' heads, wings, and bodies on background blocks, referring to photo and Layout Diagram; fuse in place following manufacturer's instructions.

5 Secure stabilizer behind appliqués, following manufacturer's instructions.

6 Draw curling antennae with tailor's chalk (Figure 1). With machine set for narrow to medium satin stitch, stitch over antennae lines first, then around dragonflies.

7 Remove stabilizer. Press blocks thoroughly.

8 Referring to Layout Diagram, stitch dragonfly blocks, sashing strips, and corner blocks together to make quilt top. Press thoroughly.

9 Layer backing, batting, and quilt top; baste through all layers to secure.

10 Quilt around shapes, corner blocks, and sashing as desired by hand or machine, working from center to periphery.

11 Remove basting; press well. Trim backing and batting even with quilt top.

12 Bind edges using 2-1/2"-wide strips of fabric used for bodies, referring to Binding Technique on page 24.

Figure 1

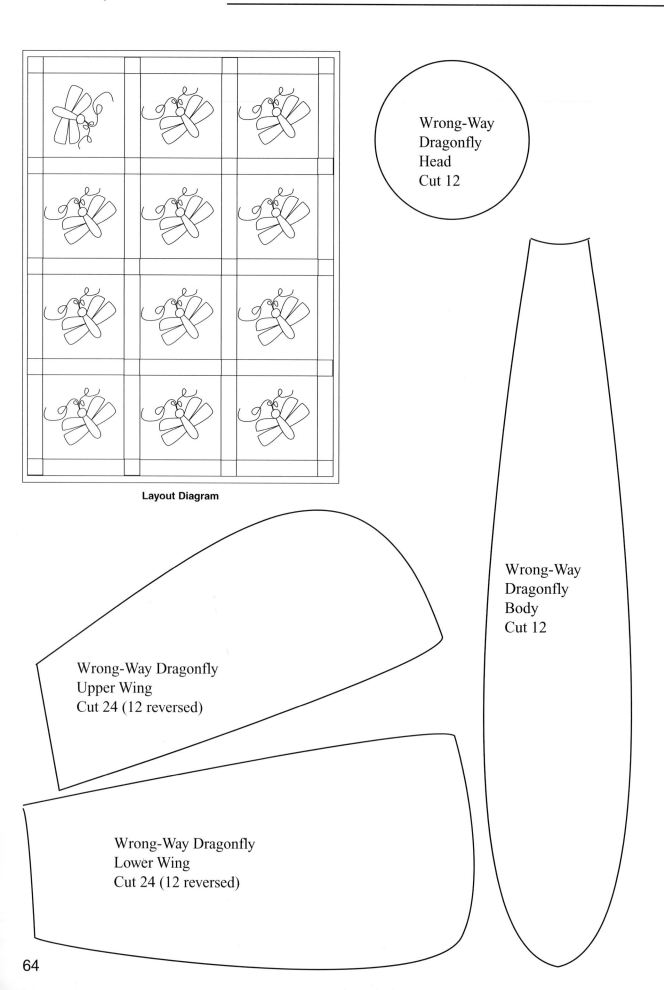

Layout Diagram

Wrong-Way
Dragonfly
Head
Cut 12

Wrong-Way
Dragonfly
Body
Cut 12

Wrong-Way Dragonfly
Upper Wing
Cut 24 (12 reversed)

Wrong-Way Dragonfly
Lower Wing
Cut 24 (12 reversed)

Large-Format Applique

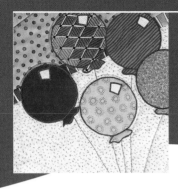

Clown Aloft

Finished size: 36" x 46"

Fabric Materials

22-1/2" x 32-1/2" piece of light-value print (center panel)
Scraps of bright multicolored, light multicolored, white, red, yellow, blue, green, and orange prints
1/4 yard of a second multicolored print (inner border)
1/2 yard yellow print (outer border)
40" x 50" fabric (backing)
1/2 yard red print (binding)

Other Materials

40" x 50" piece quilt batting
Threads:
  Navy rayon
  Navy all-purpose
  White all-purpose (construction)
  Black or navy rayon thread (optional)
Paper-backed fusible web
Iron-on, peel-off stabilizer
Tailor's chalk

Designer Notes:

Mr. Clown was just a head motif from a 1930s embroidery motif on a pillow top. I added the balloons, arms, and body for a lot of bright, colorful motion.

Perfect in a crib or on a wall, this diminutive quilt boasts plenty of bright colors, right down to the merry red binding.

**What could be more fun than a happy clown
with a handful of balloons? Sew this colorful
quilt and make a child smile!**

Instructions

1 Center panel and inner border: Cut four 1-1/2"-wide strips across the width of the inner border fabric. Stitch one strip along each edge of center panel, trimming each strip to desired length. Press with seam allowance toward the border strip.

2 Outer border: Cut four 6-1/2"-wide strips across the width of the outer border fabric. Stitch one strip along each side; trim. Press. Stitch one strip across the top and one across the bottom of the panel. Press with seam allowances toward outer border. Following manufacturer's instructions, bond fusible web to wrong side of scraps.

3 Place patterns on paper side of bonded fabrics with print on patterns toward paper. Trace patterns: two pants, reversing one, and two balloons on bright multicolored; collar and hands on light multicolored; face on white; two balloons, hat pompom, nose and mouth on red; two vests, reversing one, and two balloons from yellow; balloon, two eyes (reversing one), and two shoes (reversing one), from blue; hat brim and two balloons from green; one right sleeve, one left sleeve, and two balloons on orange; and one hat from same multicolored print used for inner border. Cut out; remove paper backing.

4 Position pieces on backing, referring to layout diagram and photo for suggested color placement. Fuse in place.

5 Secure stabilizer behind appliqué pieces, following manufacturer's directions.

6 Set machine for medium-width satin stitch; thread upper machine with black or navy rayon thread and bobbin with matching all-purpose thread; stitch around each shape. Remove stabilizer.

7 Layer backing, batting, and quilt top; baste through all layers.

8 Quilt as desired by hand or machine, working from center to periphery. Remove basting; press thoroughly.

9 Trim backing and batting even with quilt top.

10 Bind raw edges with 2-1/2"-wide strips of red fabric, referring to Binding Technique on page 24.

Layout Diagram

Clown Aloft
Face
Cut 1

Clown Aloft
Mouth
Cut 1

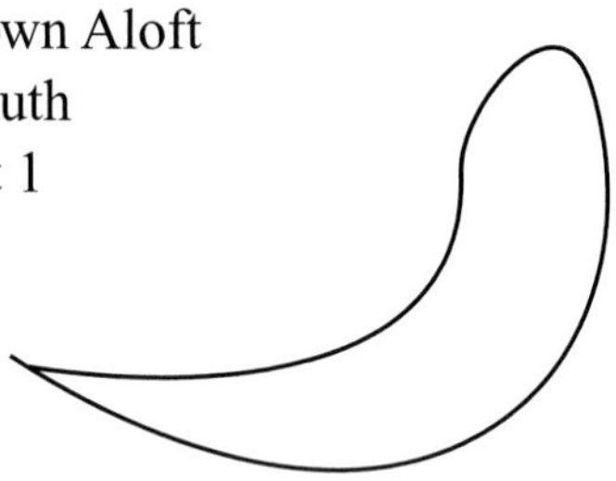

Clown Aloft
Hat Pompom
Cut 1

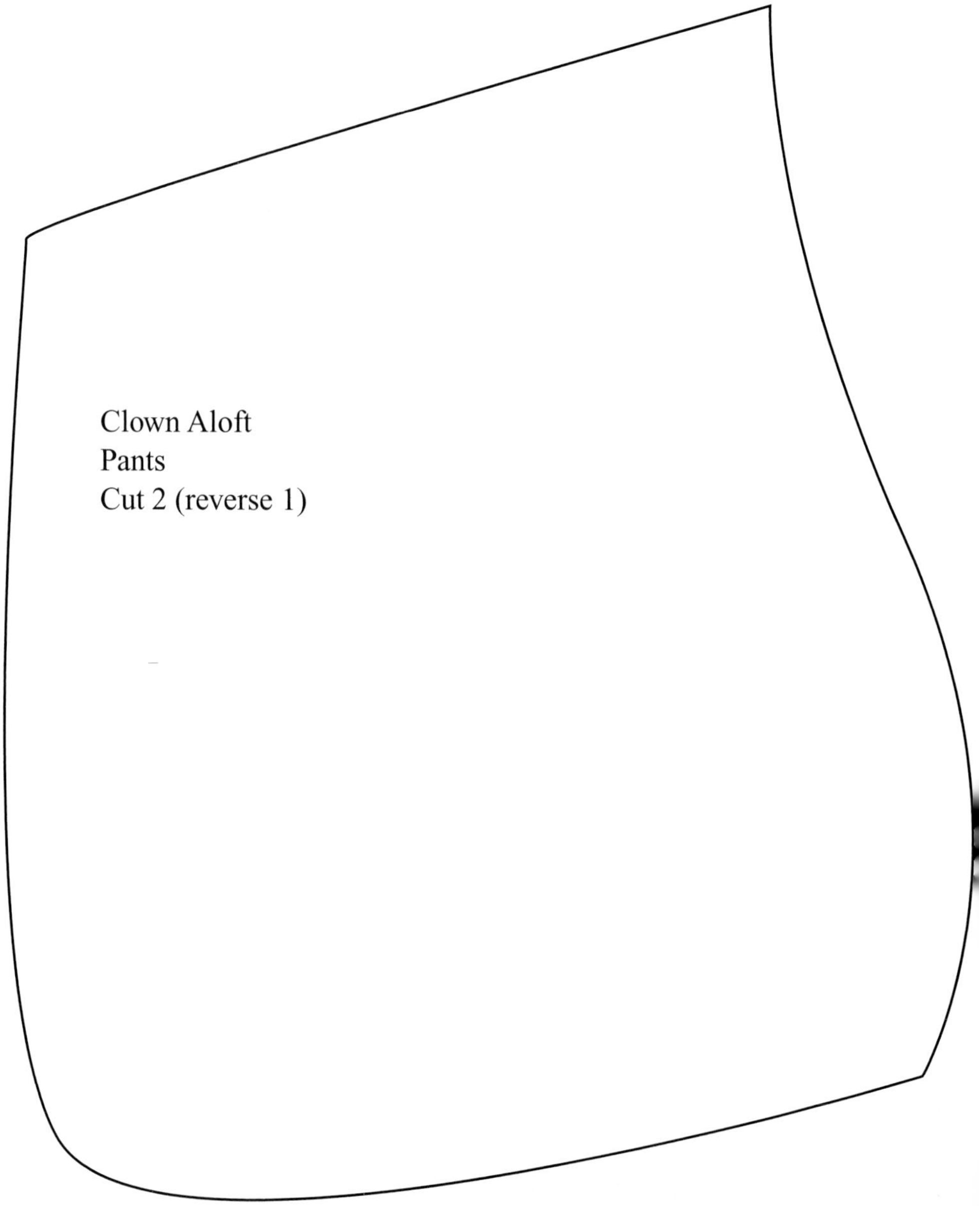

Clown Aloft
Pants
Cut 2 (reverse 1)

Clown Aloft
Nose
Cut 1

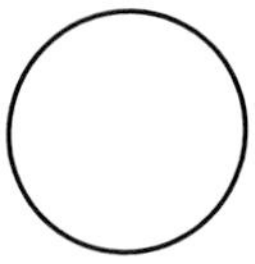

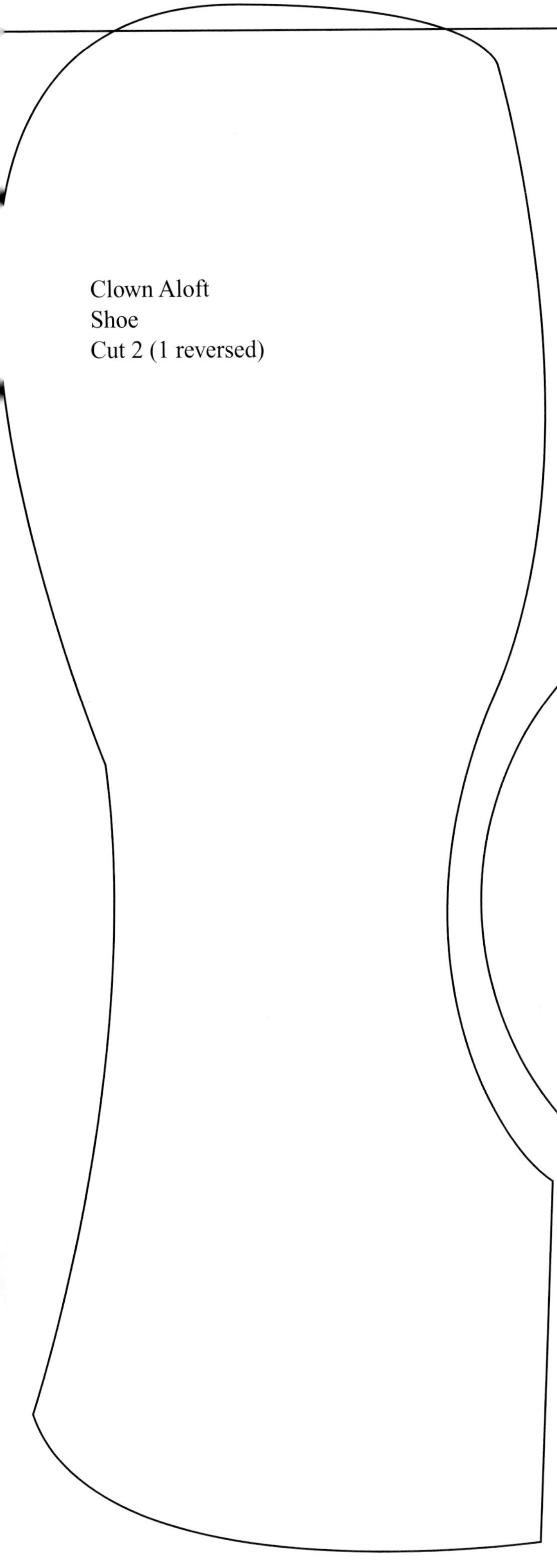

Clown Aloft
Shoe
Cut 2 (1 reversed)

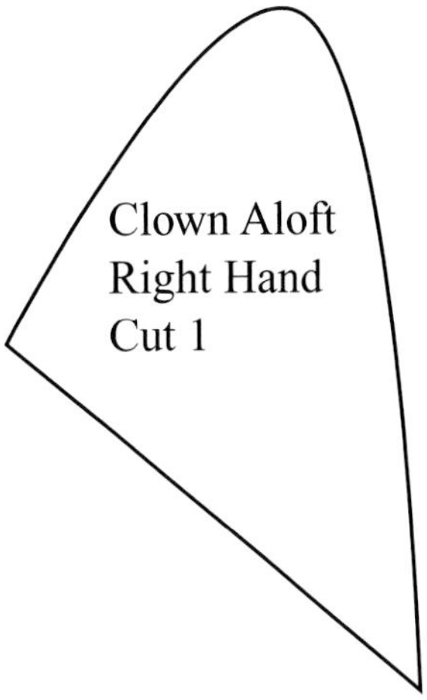

Clown Aloft
Right Hand
Cut 1

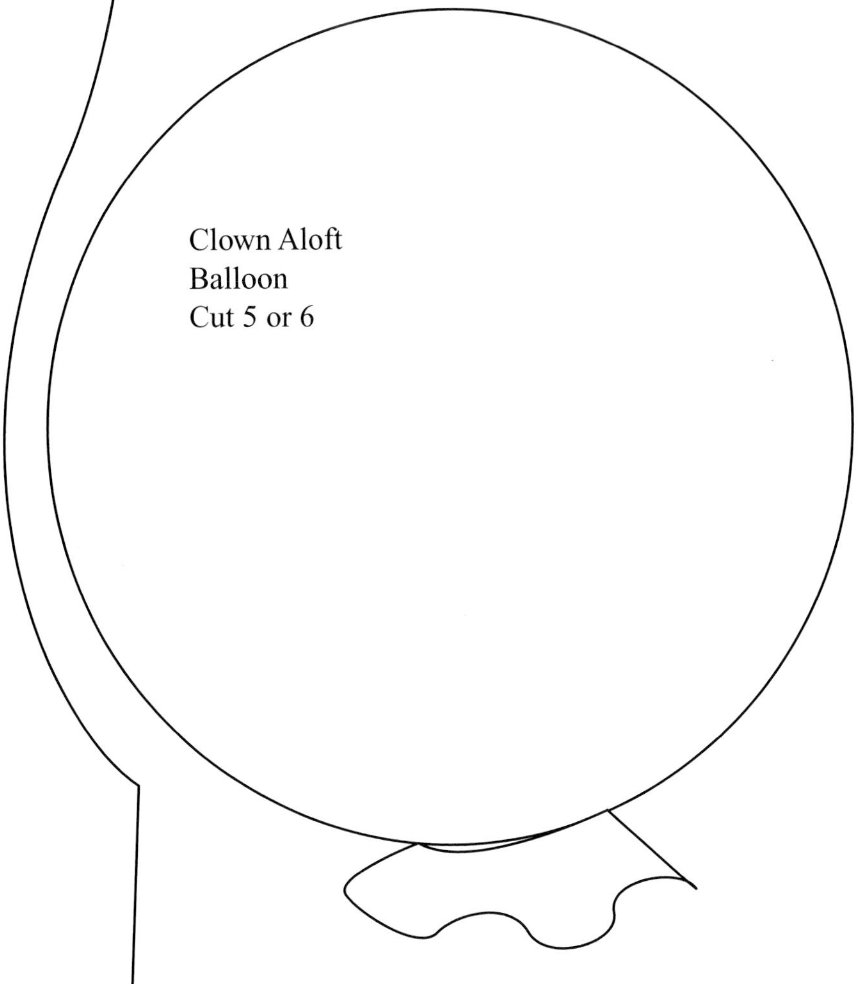

Clown Aloft
Balloon
Cut 5 or 6

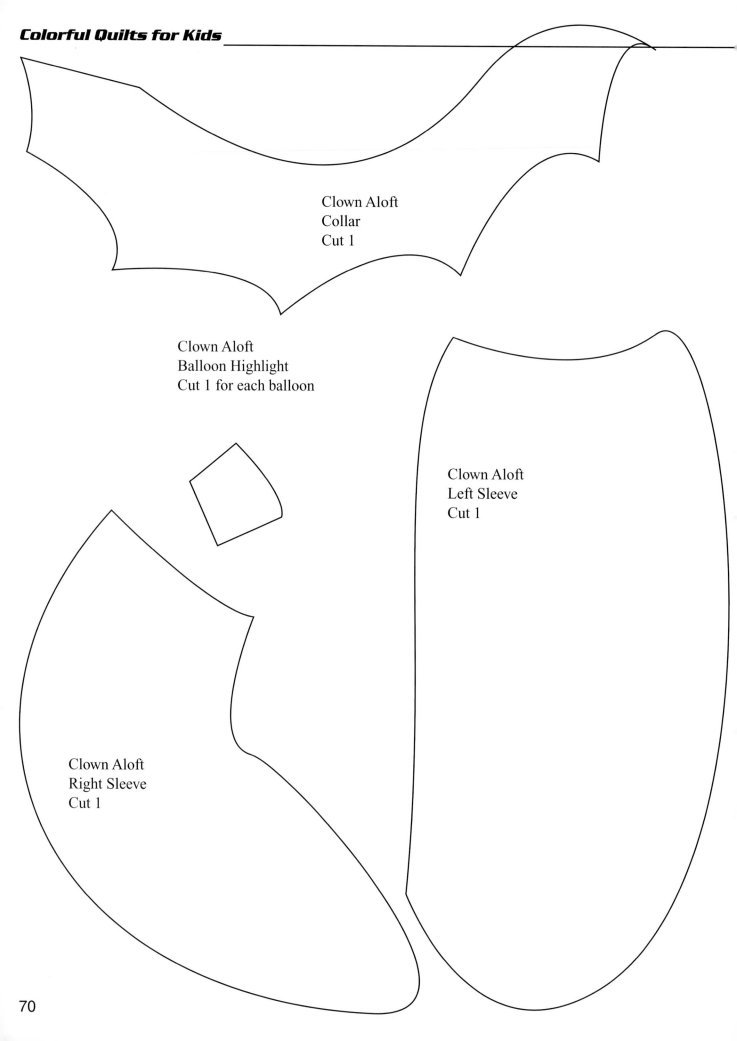

Clown Aloft
Collar
Cut 1

Clown Aloft
Balloon Highlight
Cut 1 for each balloon

Clown Aloft
Left Sleeve
Cut 1

Clown Aloft
Right Sleeve
Cut 1

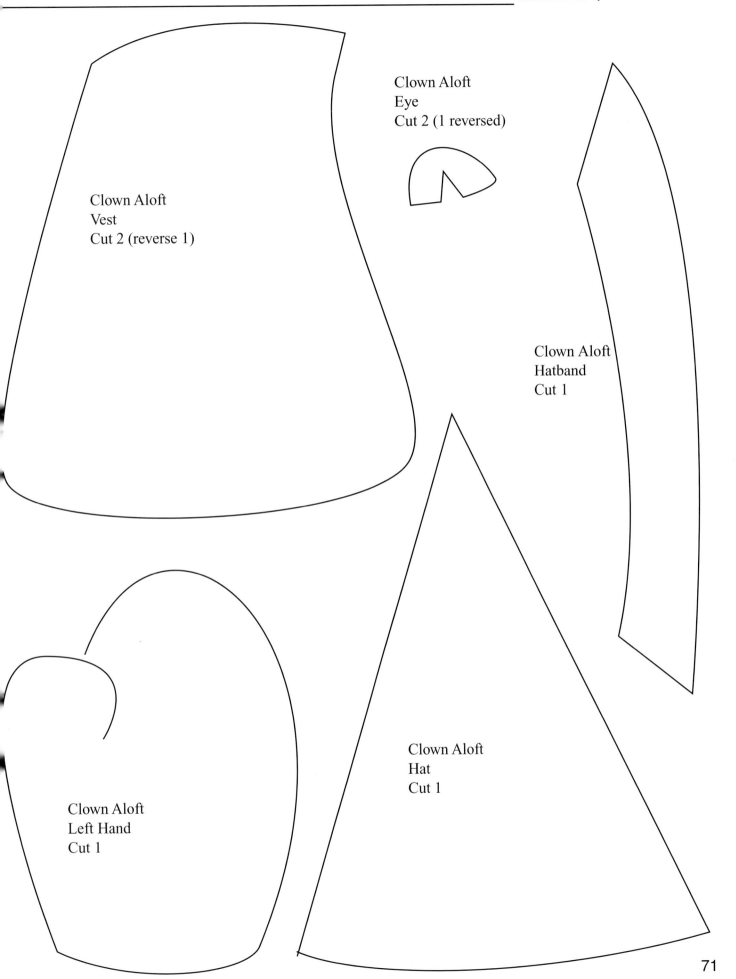

Clown Aloft
Eye
Cut 2 (1 reversed)

Clown Aloft
Vest
Cut 2 (reverse 1)

Clown Aloft
Hatband
Cut 1

Clown Aloft
Hat
Cut 1

Clown Aloft
Left Hand
Cut 1

Curly Top Lamb

Finished size: 42" x 50"

Fabric Materials

24-1/2" x 32-1/2" piece of light-value green print or solid (center panel)

3/4 yard medium-value green print (top and bottom borders)

1/2 yard green-and-white gingham or gingham print (side borders and leaves)

3/4 yard white-on-cream print (lamb and flowers)

Scraps of at least 4 light- to medium-value lavender prints (flowers and inner border strips)

Scraps of several light- to medium-value pink prints (flowers and ears)

Scraps of several light- to medium-value yellow prints (flowers)

Scraps of black (hooves, eyes, and nose)

45" x 53" fabric (backing)

1/2 yard medium-value lavender print (binding)

Other Materials

45" x 53" piece quilt batting

Thread:
 Navy rayon
 Navy all-purpose
 White all-purpose (for construction)

Paper-backed fusible web

Iron-on, peel-off stabilizer

Tailor's chalk

Designer Notes:

   This little fellow came from an iron-on embroidery transfer that was just a head. The tilt of his saucy chin was so cunning, I had to add a sassy little kick to his heels!
   We used the same-color thread to outline all pieces, simply because it reduced the time necessary to constantly change coordinating thread colors. Please feel free to use any color thread you wish — or an entire rainbow of thread colors!

Just the thing for cuddling your own little lamb, this springtime snuggler is adapted from a vintage 1940s embroidery pattern.

Instructions

1 Inner border: Cut one inner border strip from each of four complementary light- to medium-value lavender fabrics: two strips 2-1/2" x 34-1/2" for sides, and two strips 2-1/2" x 26-1/2" for top and bottom. With top edge of one longer strip even with top edge of center panel, stitch strip down right side of panel. Stitch remaining side strip to left side of center panel with bottom edge of strip even with bottom edge of panel. Add top and bottom strips. Press seam allowance toward border strips.

2 Outer border: Cut two strips 42-1/2" x 7-1/2" from medium-value green print for top and bottom borders; cut two strips 36-1/2" x 7-1/2" from green-and-white gingham for side borders. Stitch gingham strips to sides, edges even; stitch top and bottom strips in place.

3 Lamb: Following manufacturer's instructions, bond fusible web to wrong side of fabrics for lamb. Place patterns on paper side of bonded fabrics with print on patterns toward paper and trace patterns: face, curly top, two outer ears, reversing one, body, right and left front legs, hindquarters, tail and one small daisy from white-on-cream print; daisy center from yellow print; two inner ears (reversing one), from medium-value pink; one small leaf from medium-value green; eye pupils, nose, right front, left front, and hind hooves from black. Cut out; remove paper backing.

4 Position pieces on center panel, referring to photo. Fuse in place.

5 Flowers and leaves: Fuse web to wrong side of remaining fabrics for flowers and leaves. In same manner as for lamb, trace and cut out pieces, reserving remaining fused fabric for leaf-and-flower clusters in corners. Sample includes:

Top swag: Large daisies — one medium-value lavender with light-value yellow center and one white-on-cream print with medium-value yellow center; small daisies — one light-value lavender with light-value yellow center; two light-value yellow, one with white-on-cream center and one with medium-value yellow center; one medium-value yellow with white-on-cream center; and one white-on-cream with light-value yellow center; large roses — two medium-value pink; small roses—three assorted light- to medium-value pink; leaves — six in assorted light- to medium-value greens.

Bottom swag: Large daisies — one medium-value yellow with white-on-cream center and one white-on-cream with medium-value yellow center; small daisies — one light- and one medium-value yellow, each with white-on-cream center; one light-value lavender and one white-on-cream, each with light-value yellow center; and one medium-value lavender with medium-value yellow center; large roses and small roses —three of each in assorted light- and medium-value pinks; leaves — six in assorted light- to medium-value greens.

6 Position pieces on center panel, referring to photo. Remove paper backing and fuse in place.

7 Corner flower clusters: From remaining webbing-backed fabrics, cut flowers and leaves for corners of quilt. Sample includes the following:

Upper left corner. Two small roses and one large rose in assorted light- and medium-value pinks; small daisies — white-on-cream with medium-value yellow center and medium-value yellow with light-value yellow center; two leaves in medium-value green.

Upper right corner. Medium-value yellow large daisy with white-on-cream center; small daisies — white-on-cream and light-value yellow, each with medium-value yellow center; large rose and two small roses in light- and medium-value pinks; two leaves in medium-value green.

Bottom right corner. White-on-cream large daisy with medium-value yellow center; small daisies — two medium-value lavender with medium-value yellow centers and one medium-value yellow with white-on-cream center; one large rose and one small rose in medium-value pink; two medium-value green leaves.

Bottom left corner. Medium-value yellow large daisy with white-on-cream center; two medium-value lavender small daisies with light-value yellow centers; one large rose and two small roses in light- and medium-value pinks; two light- and medium-value green leaves.

8 Position pieces in corners. Remove paper backing and fuse in place.

9 Iron stabilizer behind appliqué pieces, following manufacturer's directions.

10 Set machine for medium-width satin stitch; thread upper machine with navy rayon thread and bobbin with all-purpose thread; stitch around each shape. Remove stabilizer.

11 Layer backing, batting, and quilt top; baste through all layers.

12 Quilt as desired by hand or machine, working from quilt center to periphery. Remove basting; press thoroughly.

13 Trim backing and batting even with quilt top.

14 Cut medium-value lavender fabric into 2"-wide strips for binding; bind quilt, referring to Binding Technique on page 24.

Layout Diagram

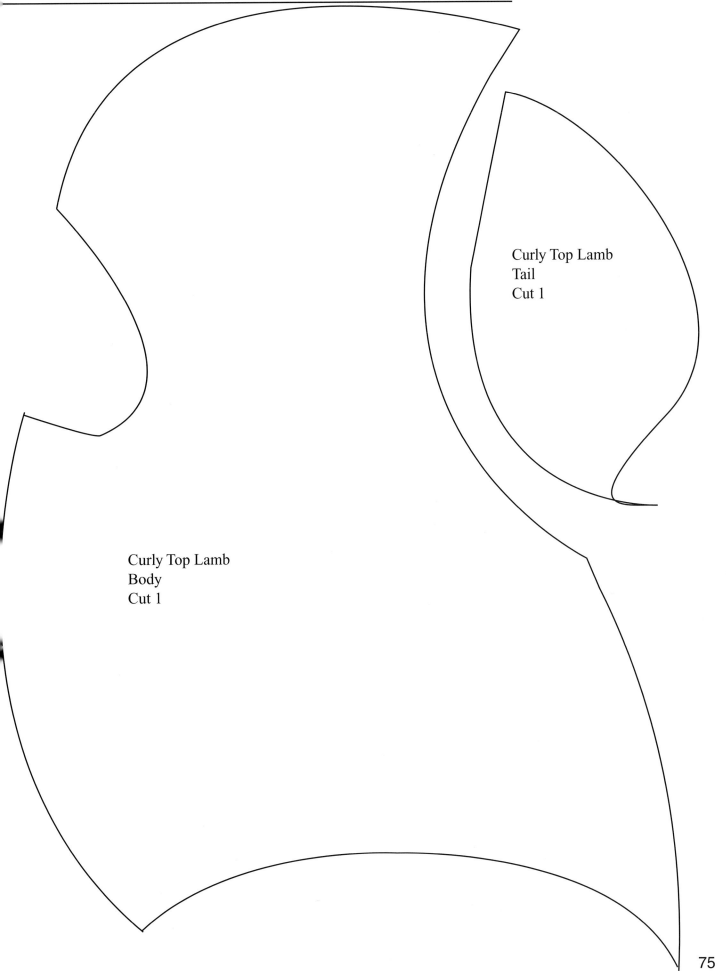

Curly Top Lamb
Tail
Cut 1

Curly Top Lamb
Body
Cut 1

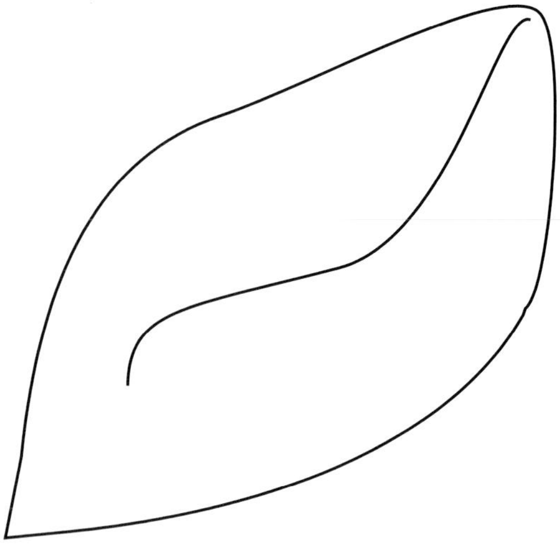

Curly Top Lamb Leaf
Cut Lots!

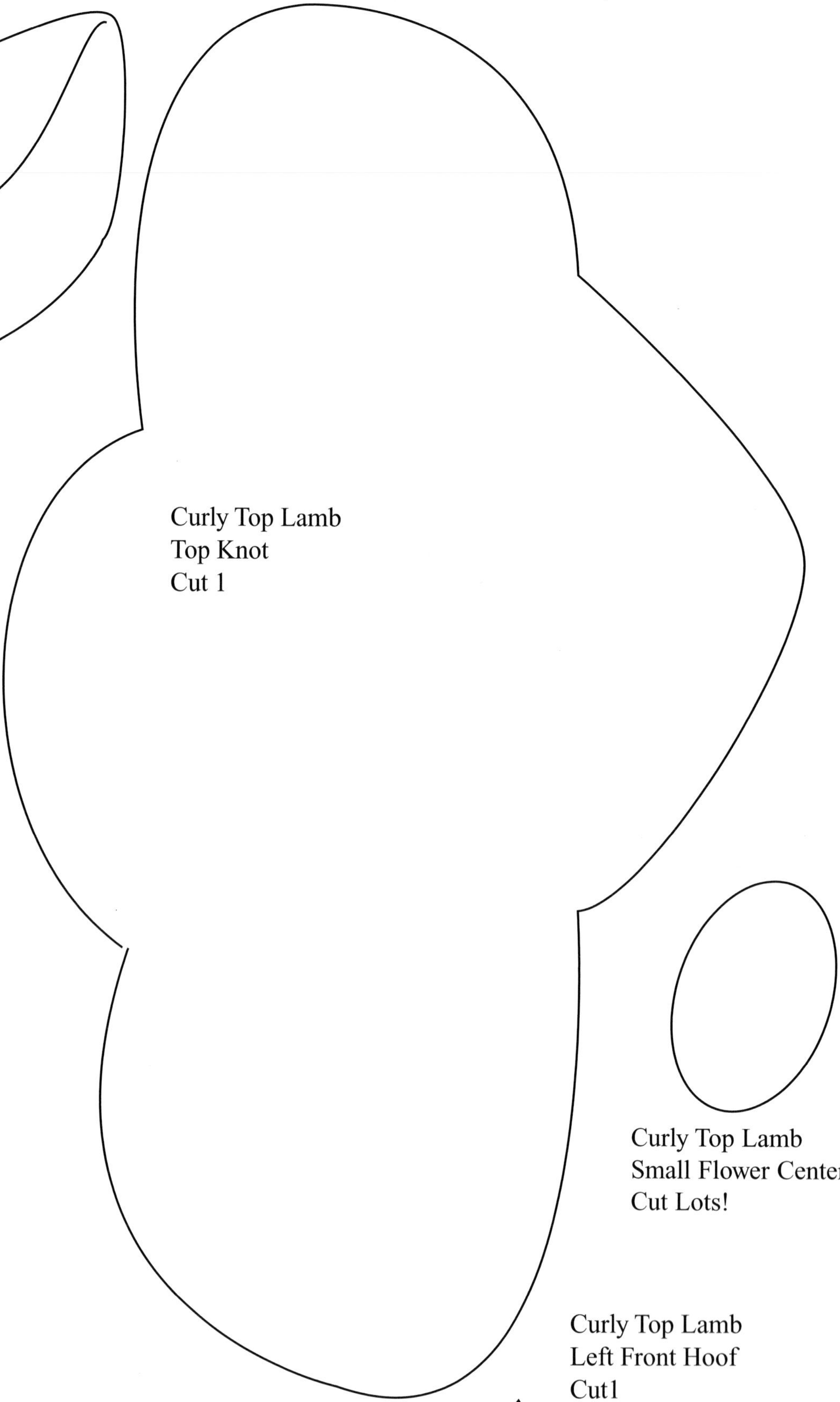

Curly Top Lamb
Top Knot
Cut 1

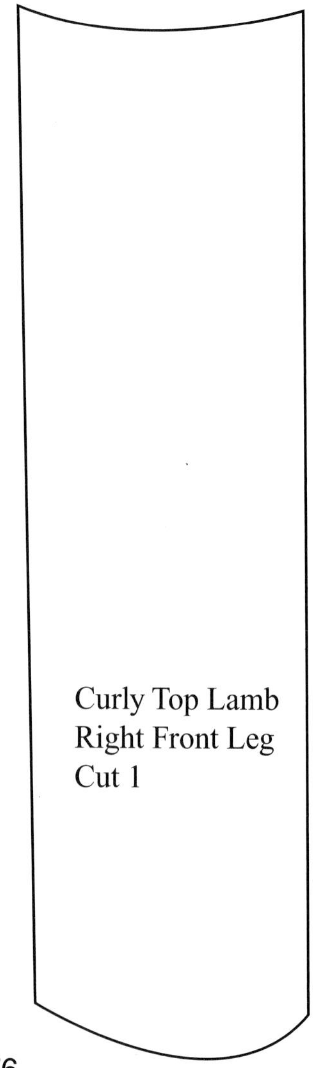

Curly Top Lamb
Small Flower Center
Cut Lots!

Curly Top Lamb
Right Front Leg
Cut 1

Curly Top Lamb
Left Front Hoof
Cut1

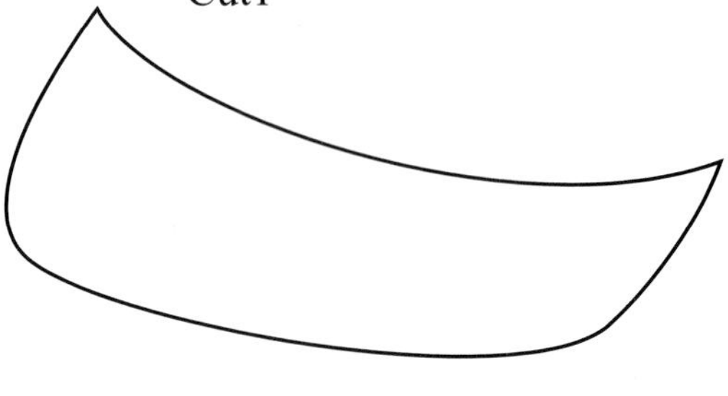

Curly Top Lamb
Left Front Leg
Cut 1

Curly Top Lamb
Large Flower

Curly Top Lamb
Ear
Cut 2 (reverse 1)

Curly Top Lamb
Small Flower
Cut Lots!

Curly Top Lamb
Face
Cut 1

Curly Top Lamb
Small Rose
Cut Lots!

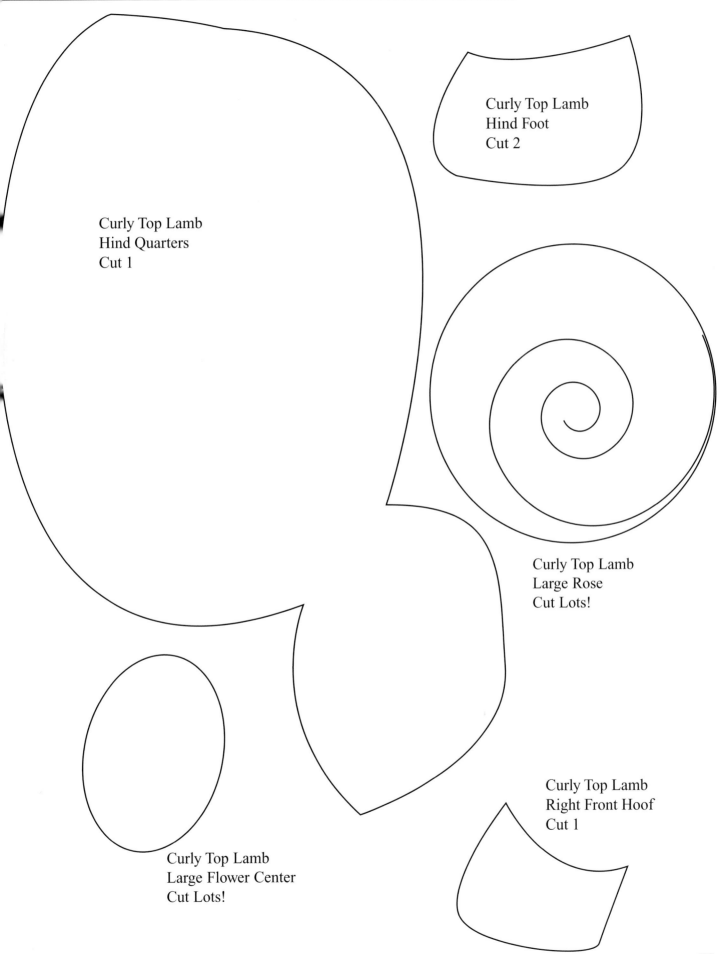

Curly Top Lamb
Hind Foot
Cut 2

Curly Top Lamb
Hind Quarters
Cut 1

Curly Top Lamb
Large Rose
Cut Lots!

Curly Top Lamb
Right Front Hoof
Cut 1

Curly Top Lamb
Large Flower Center
Cut Lots!

Elf Cottage

Finished size: 37" x 40"

Fabric Materials

8-1/2" x 18-1/2" piece medium-value green print for ground in center panel

13-1/2" x 18-1/2" piece light-value blue print for sky in center panel

Scraps of additional assorted light-value blue prints for border blocks

Assorted light-value yellow prints for sun, windows, steppingstones, and border blocks

Scrap of white-on-white print for cloud

Scrap of white solid for lining cloud

1/2 yard medium-value red print for binding strips

Additional scraps and remnants from at least

4 medium-value red prints for roof, chimney, door, inner border strips, and block corners

40" x 43" fabric for backing

Other Materials

40" x 43" piece quilt batting

Thread:
 Navy rayon
 Navy all-purpose
 Red rayon
 Red all-purpose
 Green rayon
 Green all-purpose
 White or gray all-purpose (construction)

Paper-backed fusible web

Iron-on, peel-off stabilizer

Tailor's chalk

Dinner plate

Designer Notes:

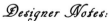

To make the sun and cloud "pop," outline with satin stitches worked in threads of contrasting colors, rather than coordinating colors.

Line white-on-white print piece with solid white to prevent background from "ghosting" through.

I'm not sure what the corona-looking line is around the chimney, but that halo effect is found frequently in cottage scenes drawn in this time period. Surely, it isn't the sun. Why would the sun be below the clouds? Anyway, here it is for vintage appeal!

**How many dreams and bedtime stories will
this little cottage inspire? Its bright colors
make it a childhood favorite.**

Instructions

1 Center panel: Stitch together 8-1/2" x 18-1/2" green print and 13-1/2" x 18-1/2" light-value blue along 18-1/2" edges to make 18-1/2" x 21-1/2" center panel. Press seam allowance toward green.

2 Inner border: Cut one inner border strip from each of four complementary medium-value red prints for inner border strips: two strips 2" x 25" for sides, and two strips 2" x 21-1/2" for top and bottom. Stitch strips along edges of center panel, cutting excess fabric even with edges. Press seam allowances toward border.

3 Snowball blocks: Cut 38 (3-1/2") squares from assorted light-value yellow fabrics and 76 (3-1/2") squares from assorted medium-value red fabrics. Cut red squares in half diagonally to make 152 triangles. Referring to Figure 1 (page 82), place red triangle in corner of the yellow square, right sides facing; stitch, then trim away excess yellow fabric leaving 1/4" seam allowance (Figure 2, page 82). Repeat in all corners; repeat on all yellow squares. Press seam allowances toward corners, as in Figure 3 (page 82). The finished block will look like Figure 4 on page 82.

4 Snowball border: Cut 38 (3-1/2") squares from assorted light-value blue prints. Stitch a snowball block to each blue square; repeat to make 38 units. Alternating colors, stitch two-square units together into two strips of 11 units each for top and bottom, and two strips of eight units each for sides (Figure 5, page 82). Stitch longer strips to top and bottom of inner border with two squares extending beyond edges at each side; stitch remaining strips down sides and stitch ends of snowball strips together. Press thoroughly, pressing all seam allowances in one direction.

5 Outer border: Cut four strips, one from each of four medium-value red prints for outer border, two strips 2-1/2" x 33-1/2" for top and bottom, and two 2-1/2" x 40-1/2" for sides. Sew shorter strips across top and bottom of the quilt, edges even; sew longer strips down sides of the quilt. Press well.

6 Appliqués: Following manufacturer's instructions, fuse web to wrong side of fabrics for cottage, cloud, sun and stepping stones. Place patterns on paper side of bonded fabrics with print on patterns toward paper and trace patterns: cottage, three windows, sun rays, sun center and stepping stones all from assorted light-value yellows; roof, chimney and door, each from a different medium-value red; and cloud and smoke, both from white solid and white-on-white print. Cut out; remove paper backing.

7 Fuse white solid to wrong side of white-on-white cloud and smoke. Position all pieces on quilt, referring to photo and Layout Diagram. Fuse in place.

8 Iron stabilizer behind appliqué pieces, following manufacturer's instructions.

9 Mark windowpanes and sun's facial features with tailor's chalk.

10 Set sewing machine for narrow satin stitch; thread upper machine with rayon thread and bobbin with neutral or coordinating all-purpose thread. Stitch around cottage, door, chimney, steppingstones and windows (but not windowpanes) with green; define windowpanes with navy. Outline cloud and smoke puffs with navy. Outline sun center and rays with yellow and stitch over sun's facial features with red. Remove stabilizer; press top thoroughly.

11 Layer backing, batting, and quilt top; baste through all layers.

12 Quilt as desired by hand or machine. Place dinner plate over chimney; trace with chalk pencil. Stitch along chalk line with navy threads. Remove basting; press thoroughly.

13 Trim backing and batting even with quilt top.

14 Cut medium-value yellow print fabric into 2-1/2"-wide strips for binding; bind quilt, referring to Binding Technique on page 24.

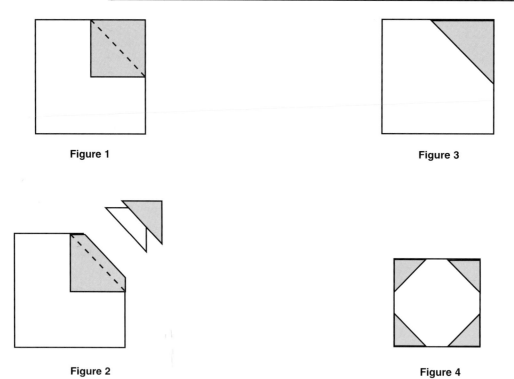

Figure 1

Figure 3

Figure 2

Figure 4

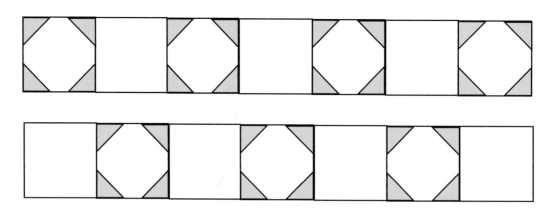

Figure 5

Layout Diagram

Elf Cottage
Lower Smoke
Cut 1

Elf Cottage
Sun Face
Cut 1

Elf Cottage
Door
Cut 1

Elf Cottage
Upper Smoke

Elf Cottage
Window
Cut 3

Elf Cottage
Stepping Stones
Cut 1 of each

Elf Cottage
Cloud
Cut 1

Enlarge 200%

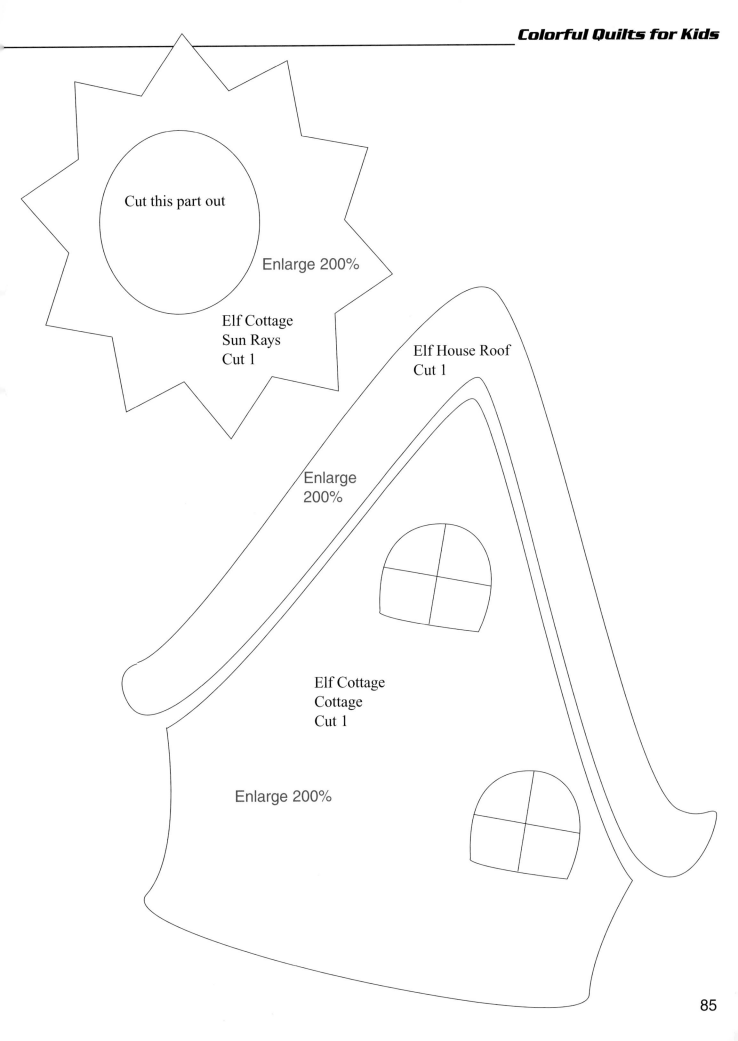

Cut this part out

Enlarge 200%

Elf Cottage
Sun Rays
Cut 1

Elf House Roof
Cut 1

Enlarge
200%

Elf Cottage
Cottage
Cut 1

Enlarge 200%

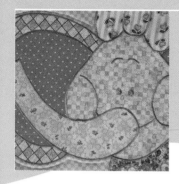

Ellie-Phant

Finished size: 36" x 44"

Fabric Materials

20-1/2" x 28-1/2" piece of light-value blue
  print (center panel)
Scraps of at least 4 yellow prints (inner
  border)
1/4 yard of at least 4 blue prints (outer border)
Scraps of light- and medium-value pink pints
1/2 yard of one blue print (binding)
39" x 47" fabric (backing)

Other Materials

39" x 47" quilt backing
Thread:
 Medium-blue rayon
 Medium-blue all-purpose
Paper-backed fusible web
Iron-on, peel-off stabilizer
Chalk pencil or fade-out pen

Designer Notes:

My mom's name is Eleanor and I was quite intrigued when her friends began calling her
"Ellie." I was already grown, but the thought of my mother being "Ellie" required some years of
adjustment. Now, I love it. At 80 years young, she is a shining example of how much fun you can
have as you age.

We deliberately left a space open in the sky area as a surface for Baby's name and birth
information, if you choose to include them. Otherwise, quilt to your little heart's content.

Also, you may want to eliminate the hair bow for a baby boy and replace it with a stitched
shock of hair.

Does it surprise you that even little elephants dream of soaring among the clouds? Heavenly blues and sunny yellows make this sweet quilt a delight for the bed, for the wall, or for carrying everywhere!

Instructions

1 Inner border: Cut one inner border strip from each of four yellow-print fabrics: two strips 2-1/2" x 24-1/2" for top and bottom, and two strips 2-1/2" x 28-1/2" for sides. Stitch longer strips to sides of center panel; add shorter strips across top and bottom. Press seam allowance toward border strips.

2 Outer border: Cut one border strip from each of four blue print fabrics: two strips 6-1/2" x 36-1/2" for top and bottom, and two strips 6-1/2" x 32-1/2" for sides. Stitch shorter strips to sides of center panel; add longer strips across top and bottom. Press seam allowance toward outer border strips.

3 Ellie-Phant and kite: Following manufacturer's instructions, fuse web to wrong side of fabrics for elephant and kite. Place patterns on paper side of bonded fabrics with print on patterns toward paper, and trace patterns. Cut out; remove paper backing.

4 Position pieces on quilt, referring to photo and Layout Diagram. Fuse in place.

5 Iron stabilizer behind appliqué pieces, following manufacturer's directions.

6 Mark eyebrows, smile, crossbar on kite, kite string, and tail with tailor's chalk.

7 Set machine for narrow-width satin stitch; thread upper machine with blue rayon thread and bobbin with matching all-purpose thread; adjust setting for narrow-width satin stitch and stitch over facial features and other details added in Step 6. Set machine for medium-width satin stitch and stitch around each shape. Remove stabilizer.

8 Layer backing, batting, and quilt top; baste through all layers.

9 Quilt long seam lines and around shapes as desired. Remove basting; press thoroughly.

10 Trim backing and batting even with quilt top. Press well.

11 Cut 2-1/2"-wide strips of binding fabric; bind quilt, referring to Binding Technique on page 24.

Layout Diagram

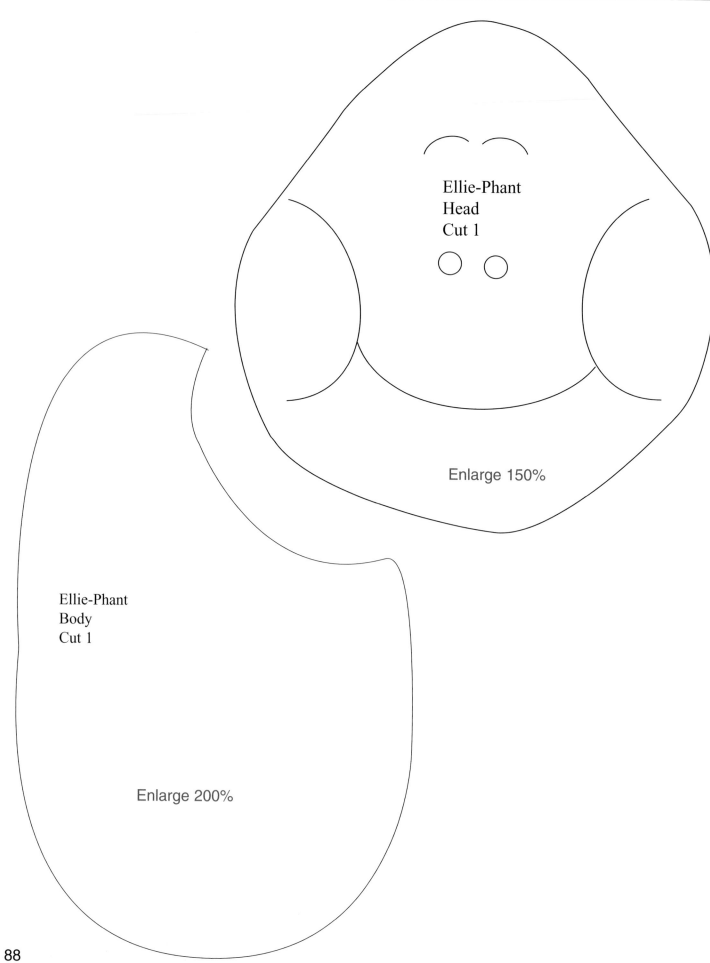

Ellie-Phant
Head
Cut 1

Enlarge 150%

Ellie-Phant
Body
Cut 1

Enlarge 200%

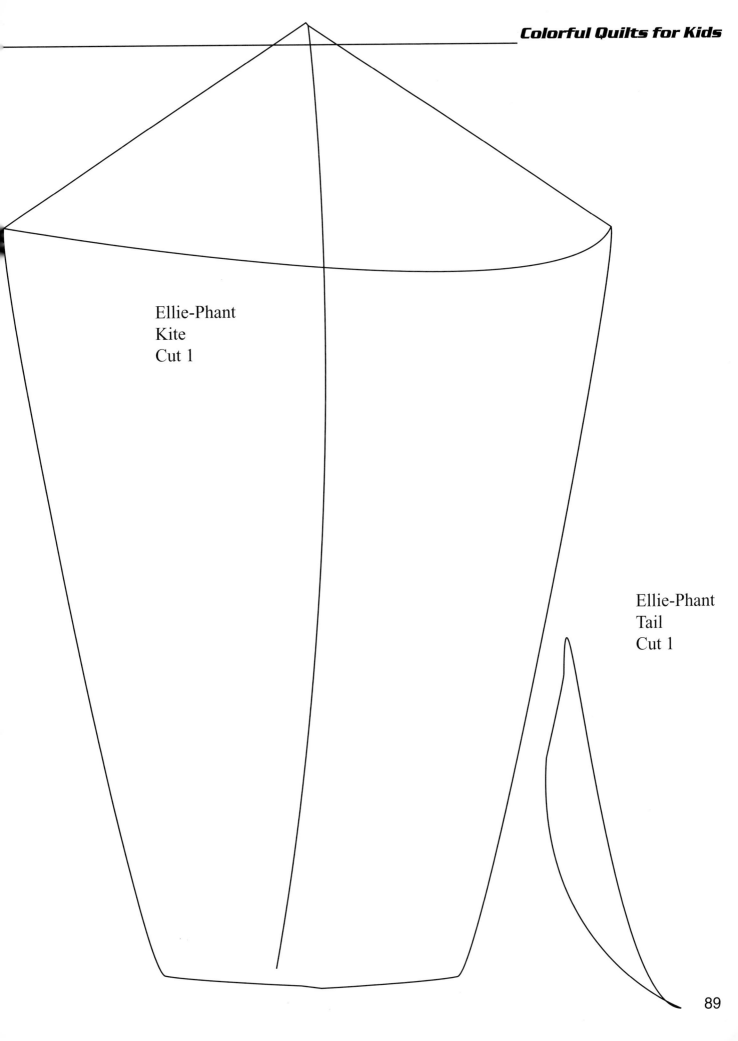

Ellie-Phant
Kite
Cut 1

Ellie-Phant
Tail
Cut 1

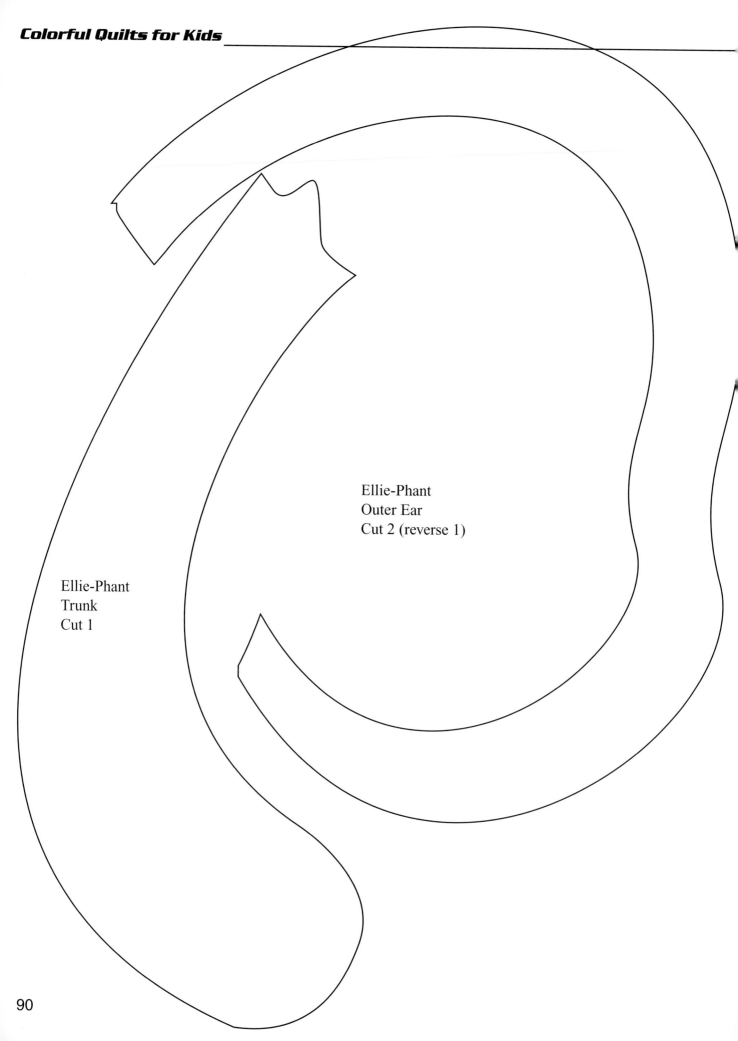

Ellie-Phant
Outer Ear
Cut 2 (reverse 1)

Ellie-Phant
Trunk
Cut 1

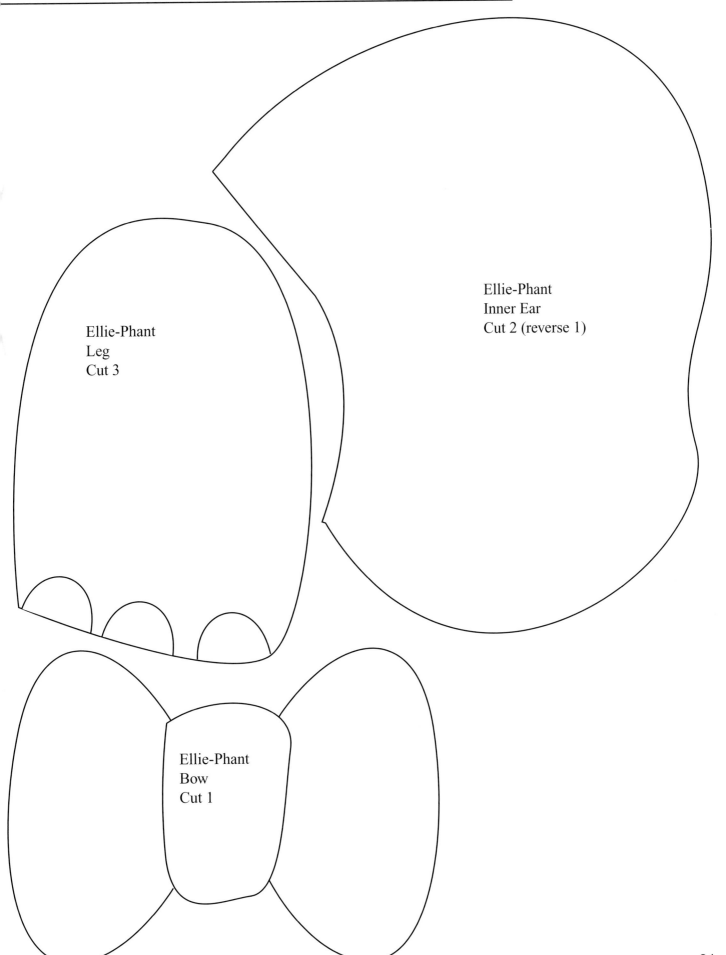

Ellie-Phant
Inner Ear
Cut 2 (reverse 1)

Ellie-Phant
Leg
Cut 3

Ellie-Phant
Bow
Cut 1

Finished size: 42" x 48"

Fabric Materials

22-1/2" x 28-1/2" piece of light-value blue print (center panel)

Scraps of medium- to dark-value blue prints (eyes, nose, inner ears, paws and border strips)

At least 4 light- to medium-value peach prints, including scraps (hair, forehead, face, outer ears, muzzle, outer border strips and corner blocks)

1/4 yard of one peach print (inner border)

46" x 52" fabric (backing)

1/2 yard dark-value blue print (binding)

Other Materials

46"x 52" piece quilt batting

Thread:
 Navy rayon
 Navy all-purpose
 Blue all-purpose (construction)

Paper-backed fusible web

Iron-on, peel-off stabilizer

Tailor's chalk

Designer Note:

   This cute monkey is adapted from an iron-on embroidery pattern of children's motifs from the '50s. I added the stylized shock of hair, crooked eyebrows, pudgy paws, and set his head at an angle for added cute factor.

Surely you know a little "monkey" who'll get a kick out of peeking back at this little visitor! Ours is done in sherbet shades of peaches and blues, but you can easily adapt the color scheme to suit your preference.

Instructions

1 Inner border: Cut four 2-1/2"-wide strips from one medium-value peach print for inner border. Stitch one strip along each edge of center panel, trimming excess as needed. Press seam allowances toward the border.

2 Corner blocks: Cut four 8-1/2" squares from assorted peach fabrics for outer corner blocks.

3 Outer border strips: Cut an assortment of 10"-long strips from peach and blue fabrics, cutting them in varying widths: 1-1/4", 1-1/2", 1-3/4" and 2". Stitch together along long edges, alternating colors and widths as shown. Press all seam allowances in the same direction. In this manner, construct four strips each at least 33" long.

4 Trim pieced border strips to 8-1/2" wide, and cut two 26-1/2" long (for top and bottom) and two 30-1/2" long (for sides).

5 Stitch longer border strips to sides of inner border. Stitch a corner block to each end of remaining border strip; stitch to top and bottom.

6 Following manufacturer's instructions, bond fusible web to wrong side of scraps for monkey. Place patterns on paper side of bonded fabrics with print on patterns toward paper. Trace patterns: face on light-value peach; hair and forehead, two outer ears, reversing one, and muzzle on assorted medium-value peach prints; eyes, nose, two inner ears (reversing one), and two paws (reversing one), from assorted medium- to dark-value blue prints. Cut out; remove paper backing.

7 Position pieces on backing, referring to layout diagram and photo for suggested color placement. Fuse in place.

8 Mark details on forehead, muzzle, and paws with tailor's chalk.

9 Secure stabilizer behind appliqué pieces, following manufacturer's directions.

10 Set machine for medium-width satin stitch; thread upper machine with navy rayon thread and bobbin with matching all-purpose thread; stitch around each shape and along details on forehead, muzzle and paws. Remove stabilizer; press thoroughly.

11 Layer backing, batting, and quilt top; baste through all layers.

12 Quilt around shapes as desired, working from center to periphery. Remove basting; press thoroughly.

13 Trim backing and batting even with quilt top.

14 Bind quilt with 2-1/2"-wide strips of dark-value blue fabric, referring to Binding Technique on page 18.

Layout Diagram

93

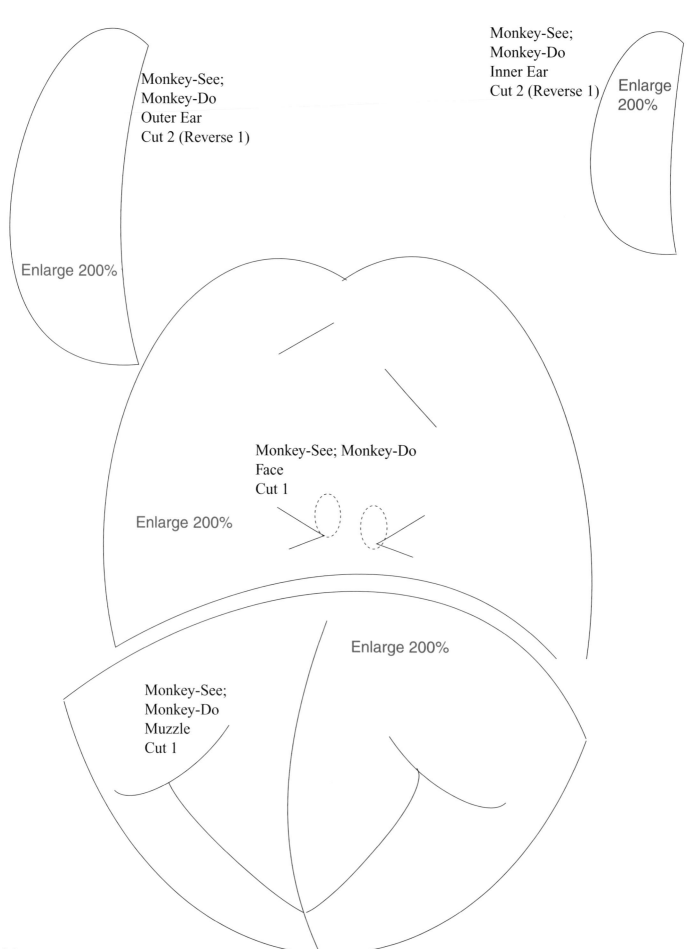

Monkey-See;
Monkey-Do
Outer Ear
Cut 2 (Reverse 1)

Monkey-See;
Monkey-Do
Inner Ear
Cut 2 (Reverse 1)

Enlarge
200%

Enlarge 200%

Monkey-See; Monkey-Do
Face
Cut 1

Enlarge 200%

Enlarge 200%

Monkey-See;
Monkey-Do
Muzzle
Cut 1

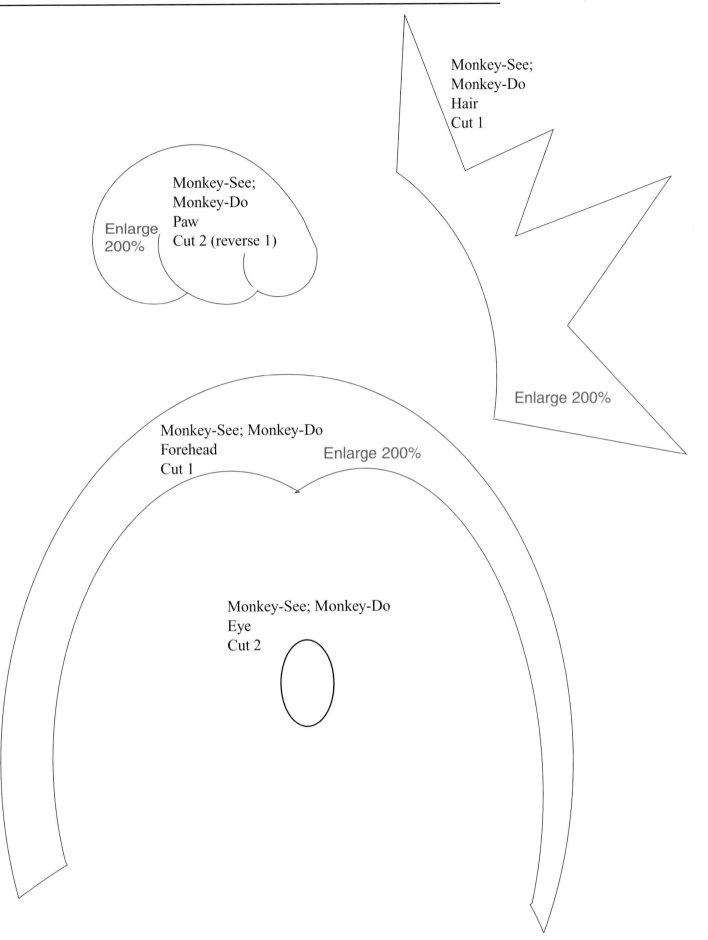

Monkey-See;
Monkey-Do
Hair
Cut 1

Monkey-See;
Monkey-Do
Paw
Cut 2 (reverse 1)

Enlarge
200%

Enlarge 200%

Monkey-See; Monkey-Do
Forehead
Cut 1

Enlarge 200%

Monkey-See; Monkey-Do
Eye
Cut 2

Pensive Puppy

Finished size: 36" x 46"

Fabric Materials

24-1/2" x 34-1/2" piece of very-light-value blue print or pale blue solid (center panel)
Scraps of assorted light-value blue prints and plaids (border blocks and puppy's head)
Scrap of light-value blue solid (bug's wings)
Remnants of assorted medium-value blue prints and plaids (border blocks, dog's body, irises, and front, and bug's body and head)
Scrap of medium-dark-value blue print (puppy's hindquarters)
Remnants of assorted dark-value blue prints and plaids (dog's ears, nose, and tail, and for small triangles on blocks in border)
Scrap of white (puppy's eyes)
Scrap pink solid (puppy's tongue)
Scraps of 4 coordinating medium-value red prints (inner border strips)
1/2 yard medium-value red print (binding)
39" x 49" fabric (backing)

Other Materials

39" x 49" piece quilt batting
Thread:
  Medium-blue rayon
  Medium-blue all-purpose
  White or gray (construction)
Paper-backed fusible web
Iron-on, peel-off stabilizer
Tailor's chalk

Designer Notes:

Pensive Puppy was inspired by a kit for Christmas decoration in 1949. I changed the proportions, added a tail, cocked his head slightly, and arched one eyebrow for attitude. Eyebrows are very expressive and often control the entire feeling of the facial expression.
Please feel free to substitute squares of fabric for the insane snowball blocks we used. What were we thinking? They are really small!

Who knows what mystery little Fido is pondering? You'll enjoy stitching this sweet topper with its distinctive "snowball" border.

Instructions

1 Inner border: Cut one inner border strip from each of four complementary, medium-value red fabrics: two strips 2-1/2" x 28-1/2" for top and bottom, and two strips 2-1/2" x 34-1/2" for sides. Stitch longer strips to sides of center panel, matching fabric edges and ends of strips and panel; add shorter strips across top and bottom. Press seam allowance toward border strips.

2 Snowball border: Referring to template, cut 296 (1-1/2") dark-value squares; cut 74 (2-1/2") squares from assorted medium-value blue fabrics and 74 (2-1/2") squares from assorted light-value blues.

3 Create snowball blocks referring to technique in Elf Cottage on page 81 or, use 2-1/2" squares of fabric without snowball corners.

4 Alternating color values, stitch two-square units together into two strips of 14 units each for top and bottom and two strips of 23 units each for sides. Stitch longer strips to sides of inner border with two squares extending beyond edges at top and bottom; stitch remaining strips across bottom and top and stitch ends of snowball strips together. Press thoroughly, pressing all seam allowances in one direction.

5 Puppy: Following manufacturer's instructions, bond fusible web to wrong side of fabrics for puppy. Place patterns on paper side of bonded fabrics with print on patterns toward paper and trace patterns: head from light-value blue; body, front, and irises (do not reverse one) from medium value-blue prints; hindquarters from medium-dark-value blue print; ears (reverse one), tail and nose from dark-value blue prints; eyes from white solid (do not reverse one); and tongue from pink solid. Cut out; remove paper backing. Position pieces on center panel, referring to photo and Layout Diagram. Fuse in place.

6 Bug: Bond fusible web to wrong side of fabrics for bug. In same manner as for puppy, trace and cut out pieces: head and body from two medium-value blue prints, and two sets of wings (reverse one of each) from light-value blue solid.

7 Position pieces in upper right corner of center panel, referring to photo and Layout Diagram. Remove paper backing and fuse in place.

8 Secure stabilizer behind appliqué pieces, following manufacturer's directions.

9 Mark eyebrows and bug antennae with tailor's chalk.

10 Set machine for narrow-width satin stitch; thread machine top with blue rayon thread and bobbin with all-purpose thread; stitch around each shape and over eyebrows. Remove stabilizer.

11 Layer backing, batting, and quilt top; baste through all layers.

12 Quilt as desired by hand or machine, working from quilt center to periphery. Remove basting; press thoroughly.

13 Trim backing and batting even with quilt top.

14 Cut medium-value red fabric into 2-1/2"-wide strips for binding; bind quilt, referring to Binding Technique on page 24.

Layout Diagram

97

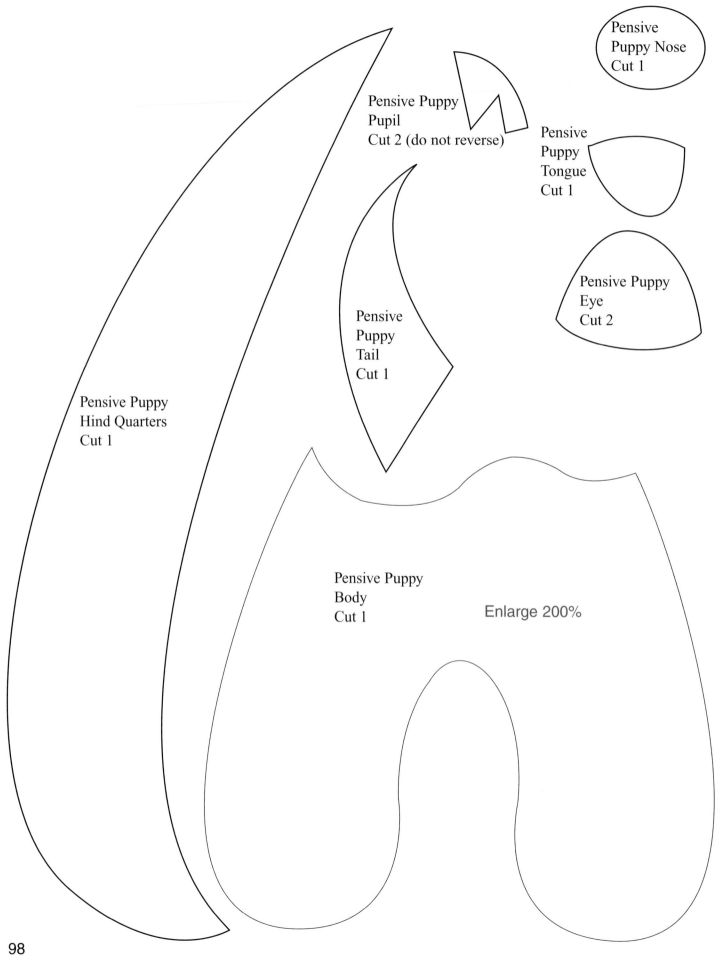

Pensive
Puppy Nose
Cut 1

Pensive Puppy
Pupil
Cut 2 (do not reverse)

Pensive
Puppy
Tongue
Cut 1

Pensive Puppy
Eye
Cut 2

Pensive Puppy
Hind Quarters
Cut 1

Pensive
Puppy
Tail
Cut 1

Pensive Puppy
Body
Cut 1

Enlarge 200%

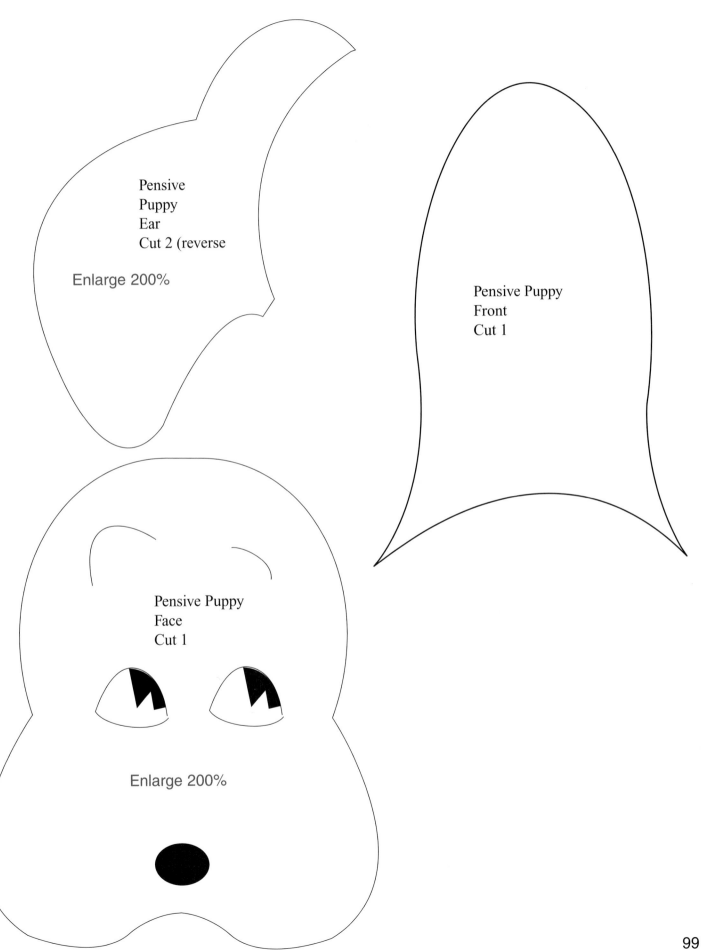

Pensive
Puppy
Ear
Cut 2 (reverse

Enlarge 200%

Pensive Puppy
Front
Cut 1

Pensive Puppy
Face
Cut 1

Enlarge 200%

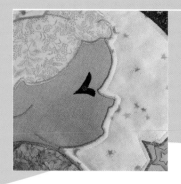

Angel Baby

Finished size: 45" x 55"

Fabric Materials

2 light-value blue prints: 17" square (inner panel) and a 19" square (for circle)

5 medium-value blue prints: 2-1/2" x 17" strip from each of 4 fabrics (inner border)

1/2 yard of a 5th medium-value blue print (outer triangles)

7/8 yard dark-value blue print (corner blocks, circle, and outer border)

Scrap of white-on-navy print (eye)

Scraps of 2 blue-and-lavender prints (gown and sleeve)

2/3 yard medium-value yellow print (stars and binding)

Scraps of tea-dyed pink (or desired skin color) (face and hand)

Remnant of white-on-white print (wings)

1 yard fabric (backing and rod pocket)

Other Materials

1 yard quilt batting

Thread:

  All-purpose sewing threads, including a neutral shade, in desired colors

  Rayon sewing in desired colors

  Metallic gold sewing (or gold rayon sewing thread)

  Monofilament

Paper-backed fusible web

Iron-on, peel-off stabilizer

Paper-backed fusible web

Chalk pencil or fade-out pen

Designer Notes:

This style of profile was very popular in artwork of the 1940s. The pouty lip and perky nose may remind you of your favorite sleeping baby.

The shape of the eye is highlighted by cutting fabric with a stylized star in the center.

Because this is a wall hanging, rather than a quilt to come in contact with Baby's skin, we chose gold metallic thread to add emphasis to the light rays from the stars.

Decorate your favorite little cherub's nursery
with this divinely delightful wall hanging,
awash in heavenly shades of blue and gold.

Instructions

1   Inner square: Cut a 17" square of light-value blue print for inner square background; cut a 2-1/2" x 17" strip from each of four medium-value blue prints for inner square border; cut four 2-1/2" squares from dark-value blue print for corner blocks.

2   Stitch borders and corner blocks around light blue background as shown in Fig. 1; press seam allowances toward outer edges.

3   Circle and ring: Cut a 19" square each from light-value and dark-value blue prints. Trace pattern for circle onto soft side of stabilizer and secure to wrong side of light blue. Cut 1" slit in center of dark blue (to make it easier to remove later). Pin light and dark blue squares together with right side of light blue fabric facing wrong side of dark blue. Stitch layers together along lines traced onto stabilizer. Trim excess fabric from outside circle, trimming close to stitching. Inserting scissors through slit, carefully cut away dark blue fabric 1/8" from inner stitching line; this should leave an outer ring of dark blue fabric and inner circle of light blue.

4   Set sewing machine for medium-width satin stitch. Stitch along *inner circle edge only,* covering stitching from Step 3 and overcasting raw fabric edge.

5   Angel baby: Referring to manufacturer's instructions, bond fusible web to wrong side of fabrics for hair, eye, face, hand, sleeve, gown, wings and stars. Place patterns with print side facing backing of fused fabrics. Trace around patterns; cut out.

6   Remove paper backing from hair, eye, face, hand, sleeve, gown, wings, and angel's star; position on fabric circle, referring to photo and layout diagram for suggested placement. Fuse in place.

7   Mark facial features with tailor's chalk; with machine set for a narrow satin stitch, stitch along lines. Set machine for medium satin stitch and stitch around remaining shapes. Remove stabilizer; press.

8   Position circle in center of inner square; pin layers securely. With machine set for medium satin stitch, stitch over outer edge of circle, covering stitching from Step 3 and overcasting raw fabric edge.

9   Outer triangles: Cut two 15-1/2" squares from medium-value blue print; carefully cut in half diagonally, as in Figure 2. Stitch to borders of inner square.

10   Outer border: Cut four 2" strips of dark-value blue print; stitch to sides of quilt top, as in Figure 3. Press top thoroughly.

11   Stars: Position largest star in the upper left corner; place others randomly on quilt, overlapping borders occasionally and trimming stars to look like they're popping out. Thread sewing machine needle with gold metallic (or gold rayon) thread; set for medium satin stitch and stitch around each star.

12   Cut backing fabric slightly larger than quilt top. Layer backing, batting, and quilt top; baste through all layers to secure.

13   Referring to dashed lines on layout diagram, mark rays from largest star with tailor's chalk. Set machine for straight stitch and thread needle with gold metallic thread; stitch rays. Thread upper machine with monofilament; stitch 1/4" from all seams and around all shapes.

14   Remove basting; press well. Trim backing and batting even with quilt top.

15   Rod pocket: Cut 3-1/2" strip from same fabric used for backing. Hem short ends; press 3/8" under along one long edge.

16   Position rod pocket along back top of quilt, with raw edges even. Stitch through all layers. Stitch by hand to attach remaining long edge of rod pocket.

17   Bind quilt with 2-1/2" strips of one fabric, referring to Binding Technique on page 24.

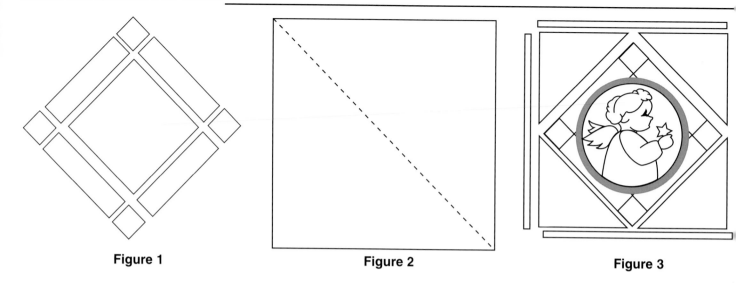

Figure 1   Figure 2   Figure 3

Layout Diagram

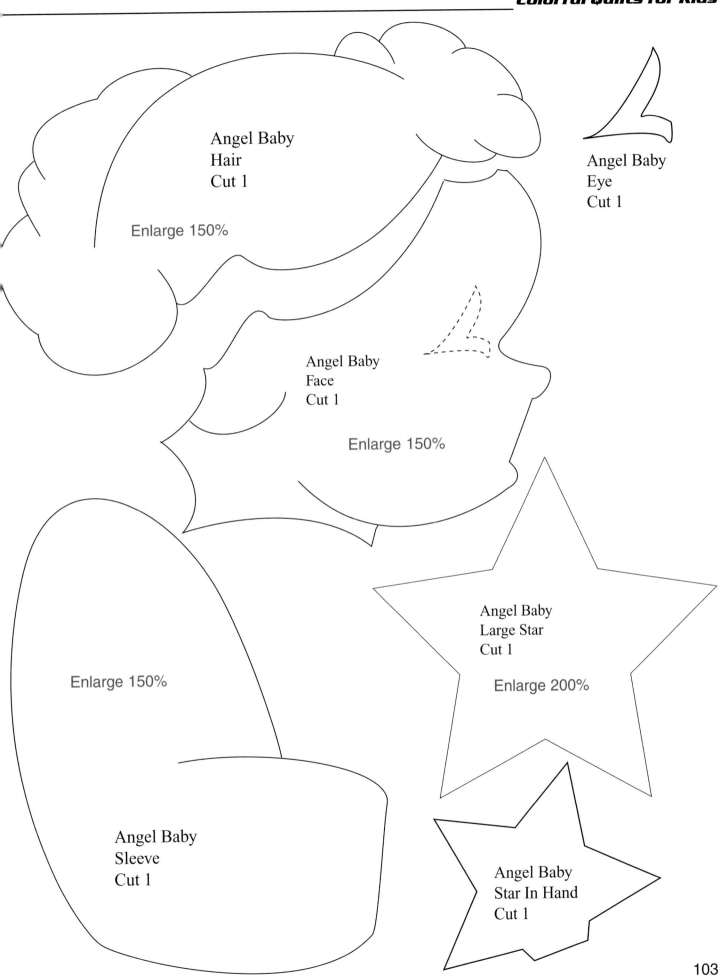

Angel Baby
Hair
Cut 1

Enlarge 150%

Angel Baby
Eye
Cut 1

Angel Baby
Face
Cut 1

Enlarge 150%

Angel Baby
Large Star
Cut 1

Enlarge 150%

Enlarge 200%

Angel Baby
Sleeve
Cut 1

Angel Baby
Star In Hand
Cut 1

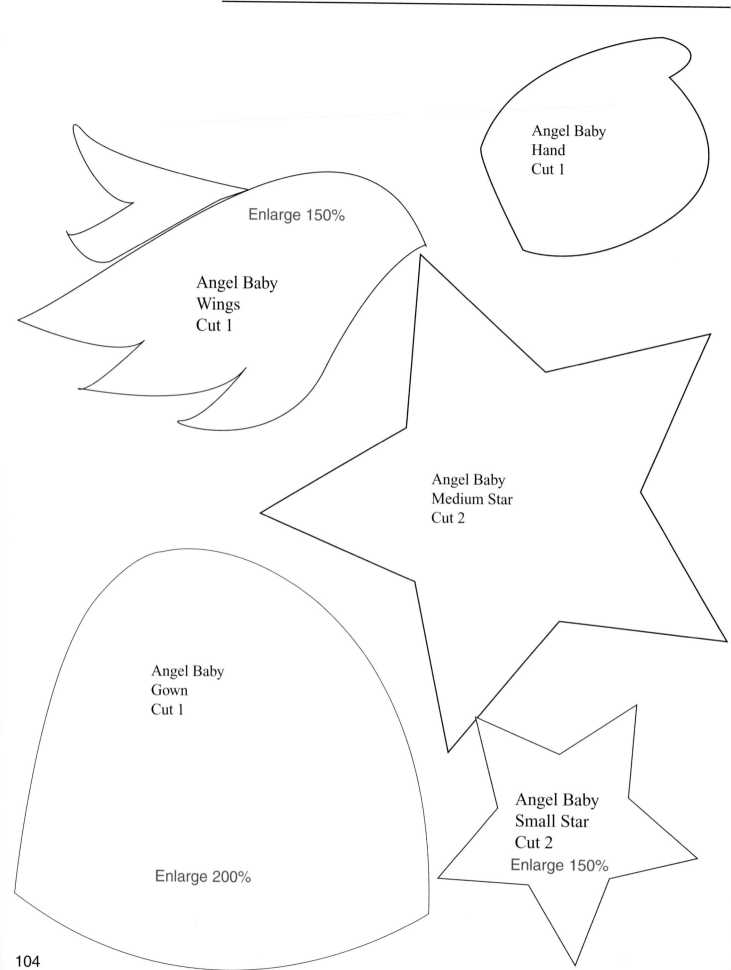

Angel Baby
Hand
Cut 1

Enlarge 150%

Angel Baby
Wings
Cut 1

Angel Baby
Medium Star
Cut 2

Angel Baby
Gown
Cut 1

Enlarge 200%

Angel Baby
Small Star
Cut 2
Enlarge 150%

Scribble Quilts

At the behest of treasured friend and crafting buddy, Lynda Musante, I challenged myself to find a way to "Be free!" when quilting motifs. I was frustrated that so many wonderful quilting patterns (the just-stitched kind) were often difficult or impossible to see. Scribble Quilts were the result. Repeated trips around the shape and the funky wavy track of the final round increases the thread intensity and surface area for a bolder design. Enjoy!

Scribble Technique

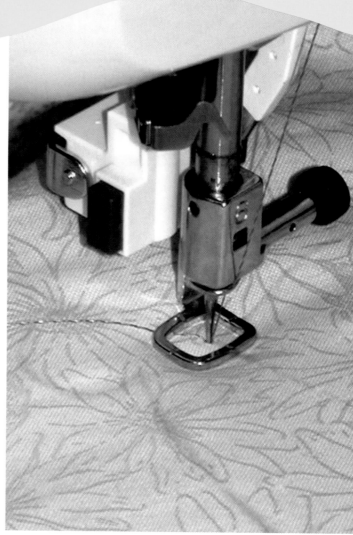

1 Place paper pattern on the fabric background; trace with a chalk pencil or fade-out pen.

2 Thread machine needle with rayon thread and bobbin with all-purpose thread and set machine for straight stitch. Using darning foot and dropping feed dogs for freedom of motion, stitch around the pattern once.

3 Stitch around shape a second time, stitching slightly outside first stitches.

4 Stitch around shape a third time, using a sketchy, wavy motion to emphasize the shape.

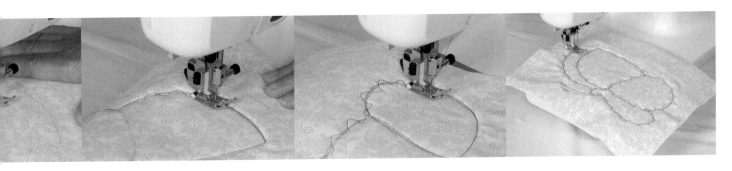

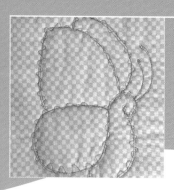

Light-as-Air Butterfly

Finished size: 47" x 47"

Fabric Materials
9-1/2" squares of at least six pastel-yellow
   prints (blocks)
Scraps of yellow prints (strips and borders)
1/2 yard of one yellow for inner scallops
Scraps of at least 6 pastel-lavender prints
   (strips and borders)
1/2 yard of one print (binding)
50" x 50" backing fabric

Other Materials
50" x 50" piece quilt batting
Paper-backed fusible web
Thread:
  Variegated lavender rayon
  Lavender all-purpose
  Yellow all-purpose (construction)
Chalk pencil or fade-out pen

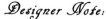

Designer Note:

I never did figure out how to stitch all three rounds of the butterfly without stopping, clipping the threads and beginning stitching again. Let me know if you figure it out!

Here's a perfect design for the scribble technique! The freeform lines help portray the butterflies' flittering, fluttering paths through the flowers.

Instructions

1 Butterfly blocks: From assorted yellow prints cut nine 9-1/2" squares for butterfly blocks.

2 Sashing and corners: Cut 16 (2-1/2") squares from assorted yellow prints for corner squares; cut 24 (2-1/2" x 9-1/2") strips from assorted lavender prints for sashing.

3 Sashing rows: Join four corner squares and three sashing strips as shown in Figure 1 to make sashing row; repeat to make a total of four sashing rows.

4 Block rows: Join four sashing strips and three butterfly blocks as shown in Figure 2 to make one block row; repeat to make a total of three block rows.

5 Butterfly panel: Stitch sashing rows and block rows together, as shown in Figure 3 to make center panel. Press all seam allowances in the same direction.

6 Border scallops: From one yellow print, cut four 6-1/2" x 35-1/2" strips.

7 Striped panels: Cut an assortment of 14" strips from lavender and yellow fabrics, cutting them in varying widths: 1-1/4", 1-1/2", 1-3/4" and 2". Stitch together along long edges, alternating colors and widths as shown. Press all seam allowances in the same direction. In this manner, construct two panels each at least 36" long for sides, and one panel 24" long for diagonal corner blocks (Figure 4). Press all seam allowances in the same direction.

8 Diagonal corner blocks: Cut four 6-1/2" squares on the diagonal from the 14" x 24" panel, as shown in Figure 5.

9 Border panels: Trim fusible web to size and bond to back of both 14" x 36" sides, leaving paper backing intact. Using rotary cutter, cut one fused panel in half lengthwise and trim to make two 6-1/2" x 35" panels; repeat with remaining fused panel to make a total of four 6-1/2" x 35" border panels for sides.

10 Referring to scallop pattern and Figure 6, trace scallops onto paper side of border panels. Using scissors cut scallops from panels.

11 Peel backing from one striped scallop-edged strip; lay on right side of one of the 6-1/2" x 35" yellow strips cut in Step 5, matching edges. Fuse in place. Repeat with remaining yellow strips and striped scallop-edged strips (Figure 7, page 110).

12 Thread upper machine with rayon thread and bobbin with all-purpose thread; set machine for medium-wide zigzag stitch and stitch along scalloped edges. Repeat to stitch all four border panels.

13 Stitch two border panels to sides of butterfly panel. Stitch corner blocks constructed in Step 7 to ends of remaining border panels; stitch to top and bottom of quilt as shown in Layout Diagram.

14. Layer backing, batting, and quilt top; baste through all layers to secure.

15 Quilt by stitching 1/4" from seams in butterfly blocks and 1/4" inside scallops. Add details to diagonal; corner blocks, stitching rows 1" apart, starting at center and working out to corners.

16 Press quilt; trim back and batting even with quilt top.

17 Bind quilt with 2-1/2" strips, referring to Binding Technique on page 24.

18 Referring to Layout Diagram, position butterfly pattern in upper left block. Thread machine needle with rayon thread and bobbin with all-purpose thread and set machine for straight stitch. Using darning foot and dropping feed dogs for freedom of motion, stitch around butterfly pattern once. Remove pattern; stitch around shape a second time, stitching slightly outside first stitches. Stitch around shape a third time, using a sketchy, wavy motion to emphasize butterfly. Repeat in all butterfly blocks.

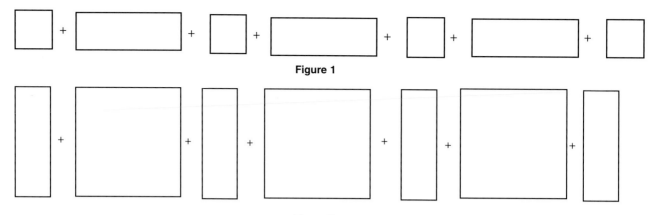

Figure 1

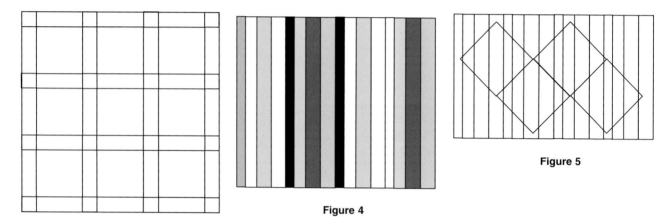

Figure 2

Figure 3

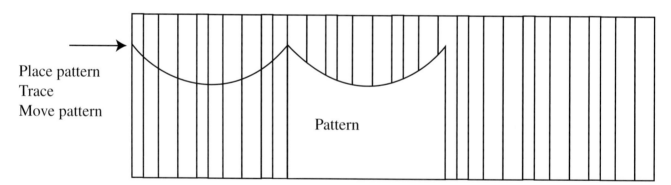

Figure 4

Figure 5

Place pattern
Trace
Move pattern

Pattern

Figure 6

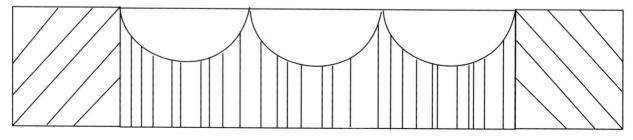

Figure 7

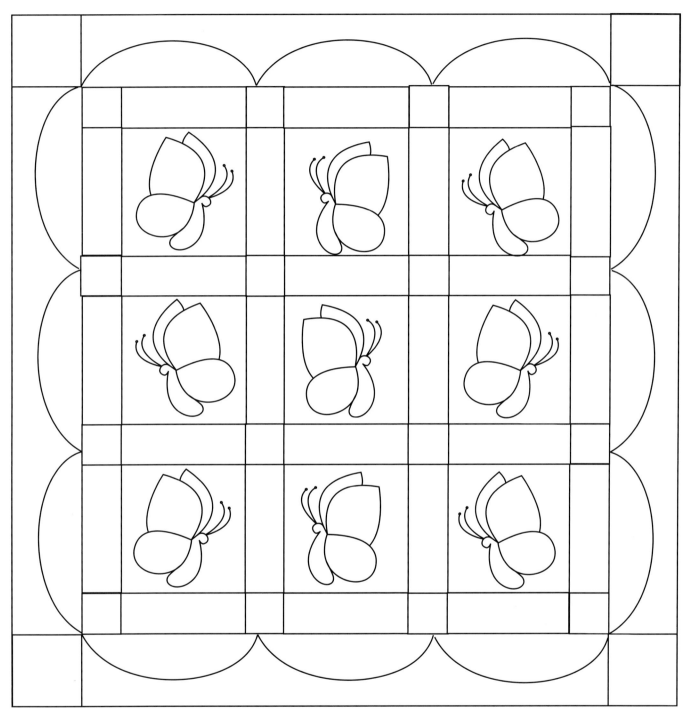

Layout Diagram

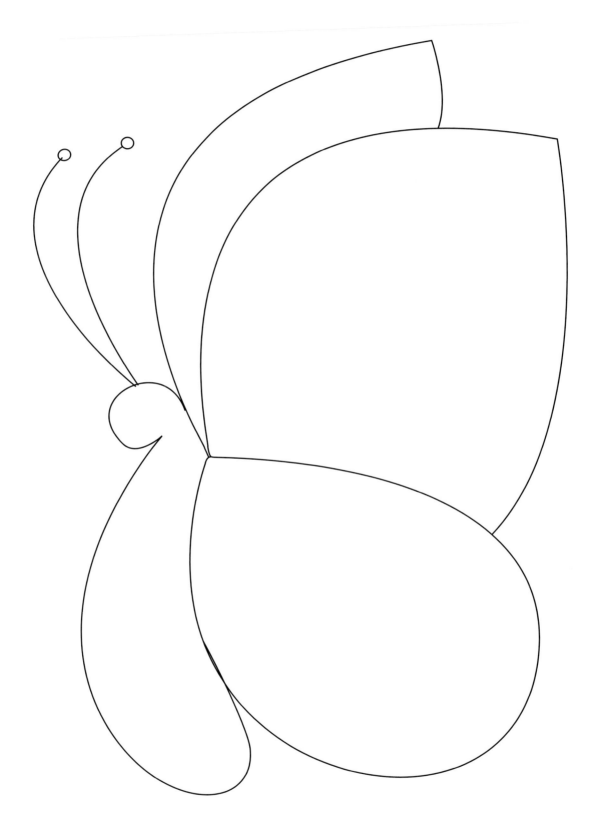

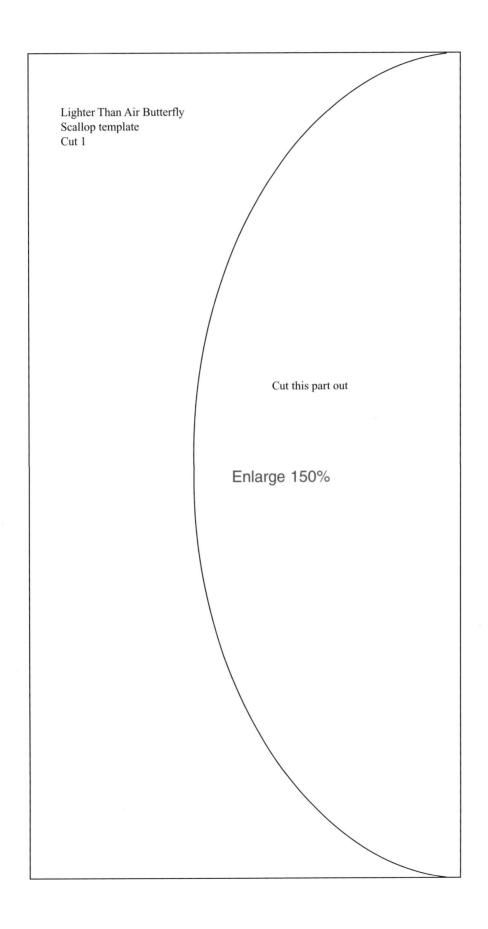

Lighter Than Air Butterfly
Scallop template
Cut 1

Cut this part out

Enlarge 150%

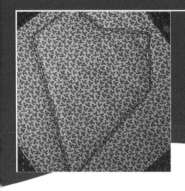

Crazy Hearts

Finished size: 56" x 56"

Fabric Materials

At least 4 light-value red prints (background blocks, border blocks and inner border strips)

Assorted medium-value red prints (border strips and border blocks)

Assorted dark-value red prints (border strips and border blocks)

59" x 59" backing fabric

Other Materials

59" x 59" piece quilt batting

Thread:
  Red all-purpose
  Black or navy rayon
  Black or navy all-purpose

Chalk pencil or fade-out pen

**This funky, revved-up snuggler is not your
mother's heart quilt! But stitched in rich reds,
it's perfect for him OR her!**

Instructions

1 Border blocks: Cut 20 (2-1/2)" squares from medium-value red, 80 (1-1/2") squares from light-value red; and 80 (1-1/2" x 2-1/2") strips from dark-value red. Working with one 2-1/2" square, 4 (1-1/2") squares and four strips, construct block as shown in Figure 1. Press. Repeat to make a total of 20 border blocks.

2 Inner panels: Cut 24 (2-1/2" x 10-1/2") strips from medium-value red and 48 (1-1/2" x 10-1/2") strips from dark-value red. Working with one 2-1/2" strip and two 1-1/2" strips, construct panel as shown in Figure 2. Press. Repeat to make a total of 24 panels.

3 Inner panel strips: Working with four border blocks and three inner panels, construct strip as shown in Figure 3. Press all seam allowances in the same direction.

4 Scribble blocks: Cut nine 10-1/2" squares light-value red print.

5 Scribble block strips: Working with three scribble blocks and four inner panels, construct strip as shown in Figure 4. Repeat to make a total of three strips.

6 Stitch inner panel strips and scribble block strips together as shown in Figure 5. Press seam allowances toward border strips.

7 Inner border: Cut a 1-1/2"-wide strip across the width of each of four light-value red prints; sew to sides of center panel constructed in Step 6, trimming excess fabric even with edges of center panel.

8 Outer border: Cut eight 1-1/2" x 48-1/2" strips from dark-value red prints and four 2-1/2" x 48-1/2" strips from medium-value red prints. Working with one 2-1/2" strip and two 1-1/2" strips, construct outer border strip as shown in Figure 6. Repeat to construct a total of four outer border strips.

9 Stitch outer border strips around quilt, adding one of the four remaining border blocks from Step 1 in each corner. Press seam allowances toward outside.

10 Layer backing, batting, and quilt top; baste through all layers to secure.

11 Stitch 1/4" from seams along center grid, in frame and in outer border.

12 Trim backing and batting even with quilt top. Press thoroughly.

13 Bind quilt with 2-1/2" strips, referring to Binding Technique on page 24.

14 Place crazy heart pattern in each block; trace with tailor's chalk, referring to Layout Diagram for suggested variations.

15 Scribble-quilt along traced lines, referring to technique on pages 106-107.

Figure 1

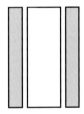

Figure 2

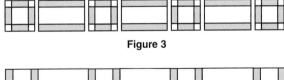

Figure 3

Figure 4

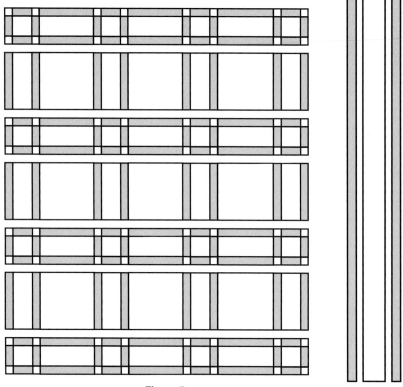

Figure 5

Figure 6

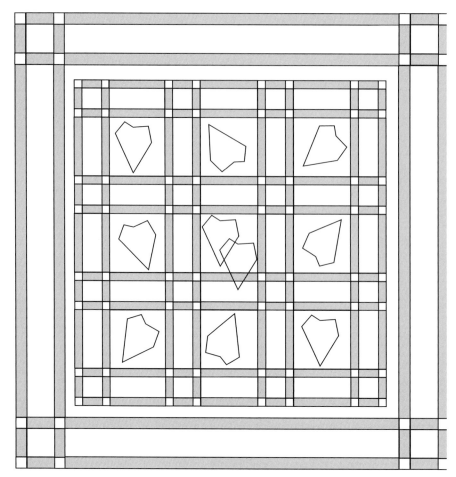

Layout Diagram

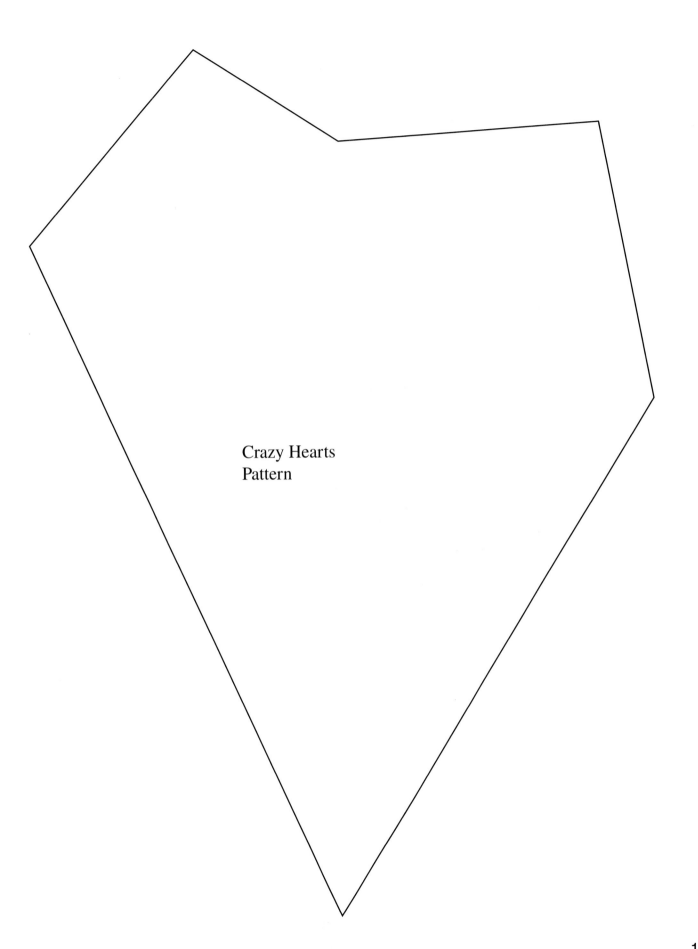

Crazy Hearts
Pattern

Sailboats in the Wind

Finished size: 48" x 48"

Fabric Materials

Light-value red prints (background blocks and outer borders)

Medium-value red prints (inner nine-patch block and outer border)

Light-value blue prints (inner nine-patch blocks)

Dark-value blue prints (inner border and corner nine-patch blocks)

51" x 51" backing fabric

1/2 yard medium-value red (binding)

Other Materials

51" x 51" piece quilt batting

Thread:
 Red rayon
 Red all-purpose

Chalk pencil or fade-out pen

Designer Note:

We invite you to use any of the block appliqué patterns as a Scribble Quilt pattern and Sailboat in the Wind is a perfect example. Instead of cutting separate pieces for the boat and sail, we left the pattern intact and drew around shapes, then stitched along the lines using the scribble technique. See the appliqué version on page 54.

Ahoy matey! Can you feel the wind in your face? Gusty breezes are sailing these cheery boats and their imaginary passengers to new adventures.

Instructions

1 Cut 30 (3-1/2") squares of light-value blue prints and 24 (3-1/2") squares medium-value red prints for inner nine-patch blocks. Join prints in six blocks, as in Figure 1.

2 Cut six 9-1/2" squares of light-value red prints for background blocks.

3 Assemble center panel, as in Figure 2.

4 Cut four 2"-wide strips of dark-value blue prints for inner border. Stitch one border strip along each side of center panel. Press seam allowances toward borders.

5 Cut 20 (3-1/2") squares dark-value blue prints and 16 medium-value red squares for outer nine-patch squares. Assemble blocks.

6 Cut eight 3-1/2"-wide strips of red stripe and four 3-1/2"-wide strip of dark-value red print for outer border.

7 Stitch strips together along long edges, as in Figure 3. Press seam allowances toward center strip.

8 Assemble top and bottom border, as in Figure 4 (page 120).

9 Stitch side border in place; stitch top and bottom border in place. Press entire quilt top thoroughly.

10 Layer backing, batting, and quilt top. Baste through all layers to secure.

11 Quilt along inner grid of block seams working from the center outward. Stitch along inner border, then outer border.

12 Press. Trim batting and backing even with quilt top.

13 Bind edges with 2-1/2"-wide strips, referring to Binding Technique on page 24.

14 Place sailboat pattern on one background block; trace with chalk pencil.

15 Scribble-quilt sailboat, referring to technique on pages 106-107 and Figures 5 and 6, page 120.

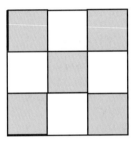

Figure 1

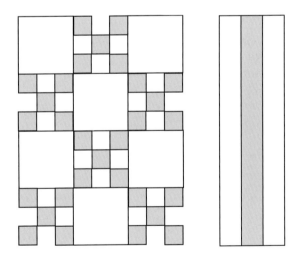

Figure 2   Figure 3

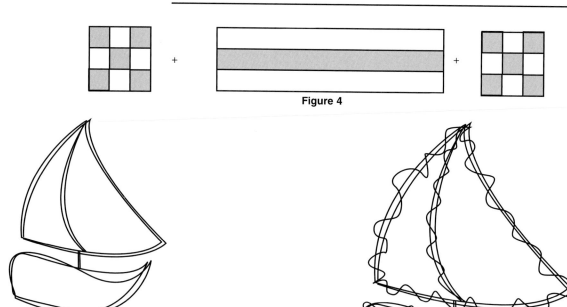

Figure 4

Figure 5

Figure 6

Layout Diagram

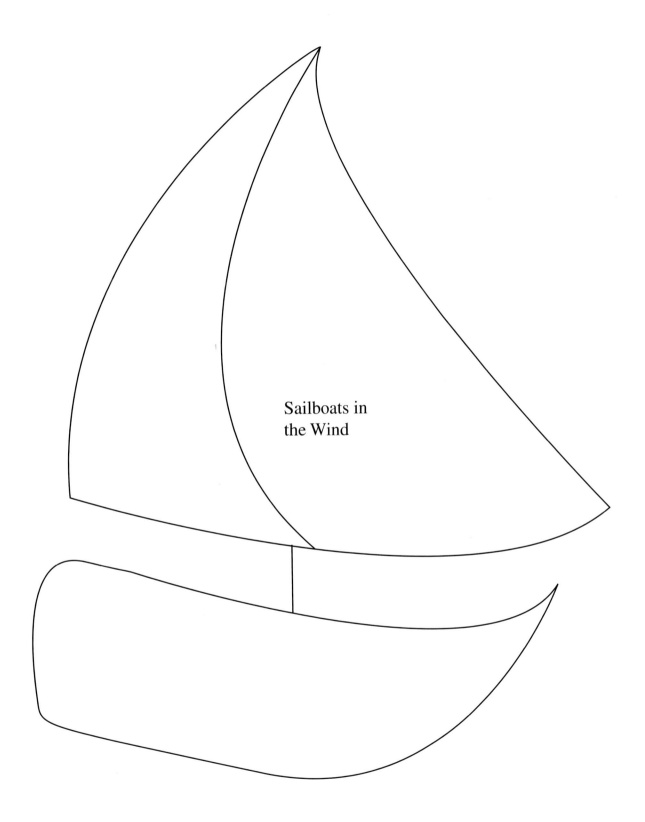

Sailboats in
the Wind

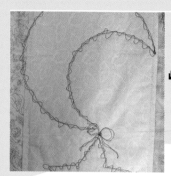

Finished size: 44" x 48"

Fabric Materials

Assorted light-value yellow/gold prints
Assorted medium-value yellow/gold prints
Assorted medium-to-dark-value yellow/gold
   prints
1/3 yard fabric for binding
47" x 51" fabric (backing)

Other Materials

47" x 51" piece quilt batting
Thread:
 2 different blue rayon
 2 different (but matching rayon) all-purpose
 Beige or tan (construction)
Chalk pencil or fade-out pen

Designer Notes:

There is something about the freedom of placing the moon and star patterns on panels, rather than in blocks. I disciplined myself to stitch two moons with the star in them, as on the pattern — but that was it. Suddenly, those motifs seemed to have a will of their own and began meandering along the panels with sleepy abandon.

Feel free to add delicate twisting and curling tendrils and freehand loopy bows.

Stitched in celestial blues and golds, this completely reversible coverlet will inspire heavenly dreams!

Instructions

1 Center panel: Cut six 8-1/2" x 36-1/2" panels light-value fabric and three 8" x 36" strips batting. Cut also four 4-1/2" x 36-1/2" panels medium-value fabric and two 4" x 36" strips batting.

2 Sandwich one 8" piece batting between two 8-1/2" pieces fabric with batting facing wrong sides of fabric panels; baste together 1/4" from long edges.

3 Lay one 4-1/2" piece fabric on top of sandwich, right sides facing and edges even "on ditch"; in same manner, lay a second 4-1/2" piece fabric on bottom of sandwich, right sides facing. Pin or baste together as needed, then stitch through all layers along long edge using 1/4" seam allowance. Flip open; press. Insert 4" batting strip between fabric strips; baste layers together 1/4" from long edge.

4 Repeat step 3 to attach another sandwich of 8-1/2" fabric panels and 8" batting, then 4-1/2" fabric panels with 4" batting, and finally the third 8-1/2" sandwich.

5 Side border: Cut four 6-1/2" x 36-1/2" strips medium- to dark-value fabric and two 6" x 36" strips batting. Sandwiching batting between fabric strips and, using method described in Step 3, attach one sandwich to each side of center panel. Baste open edges of sandwiches to secure.

6 Top and bottom borders: Cut four 6-1/2" x 45" strips medium- to dark-value fabric and two 6" x 44" strips batting. Sandwiching batting between fabric strips and, using method described in Step 3, attach one sandwich to top and one to bottom of center panel and side borders. Baste open edges to secure.

7 Trim backing and batting even with quilt top. Press thoroughly.

8 Bind quilt with 2-1/2"-wide strips, referring to Binding Technique on page 24.

9 Quilt 1/4" inside each panel edge.

10 Position patterns for crescent moon and star on quilt as desired. Trace around patterns with tailor's chalk, allowing some to cross seam lines.

11 Using blue rayon thread in upper machine and blue all-purpose thread in bobbin, Scribble-quilt along traced lines, referring to technique on pages 106-107.

Layout Diagram

123

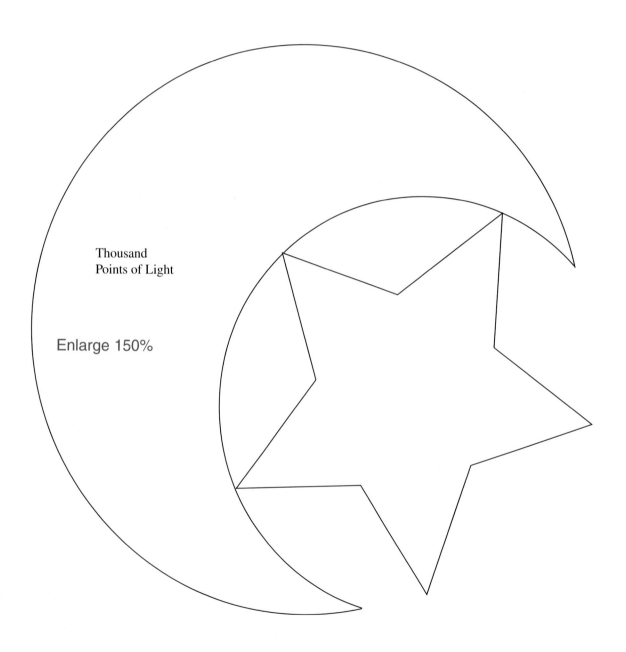

Thousand
Points of Light

Enlarge 150%

ources and Other Stuff

Dress an Angel
HC 68, Box 666
Kirkland, AZ 86332
E-mail: rutheb@sewsmart.com
www.sewsmart.com/Dress2.html
Mission: Providing clothing and blankets for preemies (patterns available on Web site); also, providing positioning devices for isolettes in the hospital.

Binky Patrol, Inc.
c/o Susan Roush
31615 Second Ave.
Laguna Beach, CA 92651
(949) 499-BINK (2465)
E-mail: binky@binkypatrol.org
www.binkypatrol.org
Mission: This national organization with local chapters donates blankets to children and teens who are ill, abused, in foster care or experiencing other traumas.

Victoria's Quilts
P.O. Box 3551
Redondo Beach, CA 90277-3551
E-mail: victoriasquilts@hotmail.com
www.victoriasquilts.com
Mission: Donating flannel-backed quilts for cancer patients of all ages; they also accept donations of fabrics, batting, financial. Great need for quilts — more requests from families than they have quilts.

Olivia's Angels
1143 Herndon Rd.
Midville, GA 30441
(478) 763-2807
Coordinator: Mary Hurst
E-mail: mhurst@pineland.net
www.oliviasangels.com
Mission: Providing clothing and other necessities to disadvantaged infants and their families in southeast Georgia.

Quilt for Kids
Unity Ministries
820 N. 13th St.
Mayfield, KY 42066
www.quiltforkids.com
Mission: Donating quilts to kids placed into emergency foster care.
Needs: Books, patterns, fabrics, batting.

Bundles of Love
7975 166th St. W.
Lakeville, MN 55044
E-mail: president@bundlesoflove.org
www.Bundlesoflove.org
Mission: Providing clothing, bedding and necessities for infants in need, including preemies and children from needy families; providing burial layettes; teaching expectant mothers how to sew for their own children.

Newborns in Need, Inc.
P.O. Box 385
403 St. Rte. 17 N.
Houston, MO 65483
E-mail: office@newbornsinneed.org
www.newbornsinneed.org
Mission: Donating warm blankets and bedding, soft, cuddly clothing and sometimes burial garments for preemies and babies born into poverty.

ABC Quilts Project
569 First New Hampshire Turnpike
Suite 3
Northwood, NH 03261
E-mail: info@abcquilts.org
www.abcquilts.org
Mission: National volunteer organization provides handmade quilts to at-risk children: HIV/AIDS-infected, alcohol/drug-affected, and abandoned children; they use the process of creating these quilts as a tool for promoting awareness, making informed choices, and community service. More than 390,000 quilts delivered since 1988!

ColorPlus Inkject Fabric
is available in 6-sheet packs of cotton poplin 16.95 + postage and handling from: Beth Wheeler Creative Services
9024 Mathis Ave.
Manassas, VA 20110
Fax: (240) 332-3228
E-mail: Mutthead@prodigy.net

Touching Little Lives
7244 Ludwig Dreisbach Rd.
Circleville, OH 43113
E-mail: info@touchinglittlelives.org
www.touchinglittlelives.org
Mission: Providing clothing, blankets and other necessary items to newborns; providing positioning devices for isolettes for preemies, as well as surgery dolls and stuffed animals; patterns available on Web site.

The Sunshine Foundation
7223 Maumee Western Rd.
Maumee, OH 43537-9656
E-mail: info@sunshinefnd.com
www.sunshinefnd.com
Mission: Helping fund residential and support services to individuals with developmental disabilities and their families.

Quilts from Caring Hands
PMB #157
2397 NW Kings Boulevard
Corvallis, OR 97330
www.reese.org/qch
E-mail: juneniel@proaxis.com
Mission: Making and donating quilts to at-risk children, including abused children, those in foster care, terminally ill, visually impaired and infants of teen mothers.
Needs: donations of patterns, financial support.

Littlest Lambs Program
P.O. Box 14831
Anderson, SC 29624-0034
E-mail: litlambs@bellsouth.net
www.littlestlambs.org
Mission: Donating clothes and blankets for preemies.

Little Angels Project
624 Trailhead Dr.
Southlake, TX 76092
E-mail: littleangels@mindspring.com
www.littleangelsproject.org
Mission: Providing blankets, clothing and other necessary items for the first month of life of needy babies born to working poor; these mothers are often working two to four jobs just to provide shelter for their families. Patterns available on Web site; angel totes and others.

Wrap Them in Love Foundation
401 N. Olympic Ave.
Arlington, WA 98223
E-mail: quilts@wraptheminlove.org
www.wraptheminlove.org
Founders: Ellen Sime & Kathryn Sime
Mission: Donating quilts to children in places like Cambodia, Mexico, and Russia (as of November 2001, they have donated 1,067 quilts).

About the Muttonhead Team

Front row, left to right: Sandy Garrett, Beth Wheeler, Suzan McKenzie.
Back row from left to right: Beth Hannum, Heidi Wiczalkowski, Debby Gregory.

Sandy Garrett

Sandy Garrett became interested in sewing at the age of six or seven when she would hang around her aunts, who were only three to five years older than she. The older girls were sewing projects in school. When she was in the fifth and sixth grade, the County Extention office would send a 4-H teacher to the school once a month and she would bring fabric samples and hand sewing projects; this fostered a beginning love of sewing. At 11 or 12, Sandy taught herself to sew on her grandmother's treadle sewing machine that belonged to her mother and has since sewn everything from garments to window treatments.

Sandy focused primarily on sewing apparel until she started watching *Quilt in a Day* with Eleanor Burns on the PBS channels in 1989. Since then she has come to love the art of cutting up fabric and putting it back together in a new and interesting configuration called a quilt.

Sandy has been a member of the Muttonhead quilting team since 1997.

Debby Gregory

Debby Gregory grew up with a mom who was always sewing something for her family of five. The first quilt she ever made by herself was a wedding present for a cousin, and it was a copy of the quilt top Debby's maternal grandmother had made for her. Debby and her mom then shared two quilting experiences when they made quilts for wedding gifts for two of her other cousins.

For more than 20 years, she has been exploring different quilting techniques including paper-piecing, appliqué and strip quilting, and thinks the invention of the rotary cutter is the greatest thing that has happened in the quilting world!

Debby, mother of three grown children, lives in

Joppa, Maryland, with her husband, Joe, and is now preparing to sew her daughter's and the three bridesmaids' dresses for a summer wedding. She has been a member of the Muttonhead quilting team since 1997.

Beth Hannum
Beth Hannum loves all types of sewing: Apparel, craft, quilting, cross-stitch, needlepoint, crewel, and knitting. Her mother introduced her to sewing when she was 11, and is for the most part self-taught in all categories.

Beth lives with her husband of 23 years and children, (when they're home from college), in Manassas, Virginia. She has been active in Girl Scouts for the past 13 years and enjoys hiking and camping. She hopes to create landscape quilts from photographs taken on hikes in the area. Her "real" job is working as a human resources recruiter for a government contractor, located near Washington, DC. Sewing provides a therapeutic respite from long work weeks in the big city.

Beth has been a member of the Muttonhead quilting team since 2000.

Suzan McKenzie
Suzan McKenzie began sewing at age eight or nine with her mother and grandmother, and watched as her grandmother handmade a quilt each winter. Her own first quilt was hand embroidered and hand quilted for her first child, Scott. More quilts (and daughters, Karen and Rebecca) followed. Non-sewing time has been spent working in fabric

stores, and in part-time news writing and editing. She has lived in many parts of the country as her family has been transferred with her Navy pilot husband, Jim (call sign "Spuds").

Suzan particularly loves choosing colors for quilting projects and watching the dynamics of a collection change as pieces are added or moved. Her other sewing projects have included clothing, curtains, toys, and costume design and construction for both professional and community theaters.

Following her husband's retirement from the Navy, Suzan's family has settled in Midlothian, Virginia, where she works as a clerk for the Richmond Times-Dispatch and is beginning quilts for her grandchildren, Jimmy and Colleen McKenzie. Suzan has been a member of the Muttonhead quilting team since 1998.

Heidi Wiczalkowski
Heidi learned, at age 13, to sew from her mother, Joyce, and was soon sewing her own clothes and reupholstering furniture. Years later, Heidi discovered the joy of making clothes for her two small sons, Ian and Logan.

When not sewing, Heidi can be found performing Mommy tasks, attending local auctions, cross-stitching, reading, or playing on her computer.

Heidi has been a member of the Muttonhead quilting team since 1999.

Beth Wheeler

Beth learned to embroider at age 5, crochet at age 6, and whined until her mother taught her to sew on the Singer Featherweight at age 7. Since that time, she has embarked on an adventure of personal study in design and color, and in the past 15 years of full-time design, has developed signature techniques for which Muttonhead has come to be known.

She began Beth Wheeler Creative Services in 1993 and the Muttonhead line of patterns branched off in 1998 with the goal of earning $25 a month to set aside for an educational fund for beloved godson, Ryan Marquette. Muttonhead has been blessed many times over in reaching those goals, and reaching out to children through quilting and crafts.

Beth is available and often speaks to groups of children and young people about "Life in the Craft Lane," and balancing the demands of life as a self-employed person. She speaks from experience — having published more than 300 articles, designs, and 35 books for quilting, sewing, and craft audiences. She is a member of the Society of Craft Designers (SCD), currently serving on its Board of Directors, a member of Hobby Industries Association, American Craft and Creative Industries, the American Craft Council, and a recent past member of the Board of Directors for the Virginia Quilt Museum.

Beth lives with her husband, Geoff, and Scottish terrier, Kippy, near Washington D.C. in a three-story townhouse happily crowded with fabrics, books, supplies, and projects in progress.

The End